BICYCLING
VANCOUVER

by
VOLKER BODEGOM

LONE
PINE

To Mom and Dad, who, being Dutch, taught my sister and I how to cycle when we were very young.

Copyright © 1992 by Lone Pine Publishing
Printed in Canada
First printed in 1992 5 4 3 2 1

The publisher:
Lone Pine Publishing
206, 10426-81 Avenue
Edmonton, Alberta, Canada
T6E 1X5

Canadian Cataloguing in Publication Data
Bodegom, Volker, 1961-
  Bicycling Vancouver

  Includes bibliographical references and index.
  ISBN 1-55105-012-9

  1. Cycling - British Columbia—Vancouver. 2. Cycling Paths—British Columbia—Vancouver.
3. Vancouver (B.C.)—Guidebooks. I. Title.
FC3847.18.B62 1992   917.11'33044   C92-091588-4
F1089.5.V22B62 1992

Front & back cover photo: *Tim Matheson*
Photography: *Volker Bodegom*
Cover & layout design: *Beata Kurpinski, Bruce Keith*
Cartography: *Lisa Kofod*
Editorial: *Tanya Stewart*
Printing: *D.W. Friesen, Winnipeg, Manitoba, Canada*

The publisher gratefully acknowledges the assistance of the Federal Department of Communications, Alberta Culture and Multiculturalism, the Canada Council, and the Alberta Foundation for the Arts in the production of this book.

CONTENTS

RICHMOND & DELTA

DISCLAIMER

The author believes the cycling routes in this book to be accurately and fairly described. However, cycling, whether on the road or on trails, does entail certain risks to the rider and the bicycle. It remains the duty of the user of this book to assume responsibility for determining which routes, roads, trails, paths, and prevailing conditions are in fact appropriate for her/his riding skills and equipment, and to operate the bicycle in a prudent manner that will ensure the safety of both the user and other parties, be they motorists, pedestrians, cyclists, equestrians, or otherwise.

A WORD OF THANKS

Although I am listed as the author of this book, many other people also deserve a share of the credit. In the first place, this book would never have come about were it not for the contagious enthusiasm and encouragement of Shane Kennedy. Likewise, it would have been far less comprehensive without the generous help of many other individuals.

I'd like to thank everyone who helped make this book possible (though of course the blame for any errors must come to rest on my own shoulders), specifically

• The engineers, planners, administrators, other staff members, and consultants who responded to my inquiries about bicycle routes and facilities within their jurisdictions: Michelle Blake, Robert Brennan, Don Brynildsen, Jim Cuthbert, Neal Dockendorf, Dave Gibson, Steve Kautz, Peter Malcolm, Jim Marsh, Marty McEachern, Gord McKay, Keith Ross, Laura Ryan, Yvonne Stich, Mark Zaborniak, and several people whose names I neglected to record; those with the Greater Vancouver Regional District: Jim Chim, Gordon Smith, and Joe Stott; and those with (or working on projects for) Ministry of Transportation and Highways: Sam Brand, Ron Gratz, Greg Iwasko, Menno Martins, Ken McDonald, and Grant Smith;

• My cycling friends, who shared my excitement, made useful suggestions, rode with me, or went out of their way to pose for photos, including Michel Desrochers, Don Furseth, Parvaneh Furseth, Thomas Furseth, Jason Hartley, Sarah Khan, Aubrey Nealon, Ian Parfitt, Marilyn Pollard, Sally Smith, Grant Watson, "The Bicycle People," and also the other riders who, knowingly or not, also appear in photos;

• The racers, advocates, professional cyclists, Bicycling Association of BC staff, and others who provided valuable information regarding particular aspects of cycling, including Peter Aram, Erling Grenager, Jeff Hohner, Ross Kirkwood, Danelle Laidlaw, Dean McKay, Pura Noriega, Trish Sinclair, Betty Third, and John Whistler;

• The people who provided other enriching information regarding routes and highlights: Jim Burgess, Patricia Kilt, Mike Levenston, Archie Miller, Wayne Odermat, Eric Veale, Jim Wolf, the staff at the Vancouver Public Library, numerous authors of other books, and many other folks I encountered along the way;

• And finally, my supportive and understanding friends at Lone Pine Publishing who used their skills and diligent efforts to turn a manuscript into a book: Lisa Kofod, Tanya Stewart, and Beata Kurpinski.

Introduction

"Isn't life tough enough without riding one of those damn things?" I was momentarily speechless. The elderly gentleman was referring to my bicycle, which I had just unlocked in front of a bank on Vancouver's Fraser Street. He doubtless had my best interests at heart, but we had a definite difference in outlook. Caught with my eloquence down, I had a brief chat with the man, but I suspect he remained convinced of his original opinion.

Although a few sceptics continue to view the bicycle as some kind of a toy and a dangerous one at that, it is in fact a legitimate vehicle, both elegant and highly efficient. Versatile, well-suited to both transportation and recreation, and with an especially strong appeal to anyone with environmental or fitness concerns, it is a true "freedom machine" if ever there was one. Besides, cycling is just plain fun.

This is primarily a guidebook to get you to some of the most pleasant cycling and most interesting attractions from Horseshoe Bay east to New Westminster and Delta. Moreover, supplementary sections offer tips on clothing, equipment, safety, and food, while others provide insight into various kinds of bicycle racing, what it's like to be a bicycle courier, the bicycle as transportation, and so on. Finally, there are reference sections to give you guidance on such topics as finding your way across bridges, who's doing what to make the streets more bicycle-friendly, and clubs to join.

If you've lived in the Greater Vancouver for any length of time, you already know that there's a lot to explore out there (if not, you'll soon find out) and what better way to do so than on a bicycle?

Although there are 32 routes to choose from in this book, you're bound to want to find further places to cycle. Closest at hand are other Lower Mainland roads not covered in this book, especially in Langley, Matsqui, Abbotsford, and Chilliwack, but also through Mission, Maple Ridge, Surrey, and more urban areas.

For longer trips, the Gulf Islands make for great cycling, or try Bowen Island. Many Lower Mainland cyclists also head south into Washington State on occasion.

SO WHAT'S SO GREAT ABOUT THESE ROUTES?

Some routes are flat, some have steep climbs. Some are long, others short. On one you might be steeped in history, while another will take you where the grass is greener and the blackberries sweeter. An underlying assumption is that you're looking for somewhere the cars haven't discovered, or at least where they aren't at their noisiest, smelliest, and most dangerous. In all cases these routes have been designed to be interesting and fun.

RIGHT: These routes will show you beautiful vistas beyond compare.

This book adopts a decentralized approach, with start/end points distributed throughout the area, not just in downtown Vancouver. In addition, the wide range of lengths, elevation gains, and highlights assures that there is something to appeal to people of different abilities and interests.

You need not ride these routes exactly as described. Feel free to begin any of them at a place other than the suggested starting point, or to only ride certain sections. Most of these routes can also be ridden in reverse order, but you may have occasional difficulties with one-way roads, trickier left turns, lower anticipation levels, and steeper hill climbs. Stronger or more ambitious cyclists may want to combine two or more routes for a longer ride.

In many cases you'll want to ride right from your home to the route's starting point. On those occasions when driving to the beginning seems appropriate, you'll usually find some kind of parking nearby; many routes begin at parks, community centres, and schools.

Most of these routes can be ridden on any geared bike in good working order, some are just fine on a one-speed, while others are best experienced on a mountain bike.

Although crossings of busy roads are generally at a traffic light, in some cases you'll have to push the pedestrian crosswalk button to get through; sometimes, however, you won't even be that lucky.

USING THE DESCRIPTIONS

The route descriptions are in four parts: a map, an information summary, a road log, and a few paragraph of descriptive prose.

The maps are all quite detailed and show most (but not all), streets in the vicinity of the route. However, there is only enough space to show a few of the points of interest associated with each route, so the road log will be a valuable companion.

LEGEND

———	Bike Route- paved roads	— - - -	International Boundary
— — -	Bike Route- gravel roads	———	Park Outline
Ⓢ	Start of Bike Route	··············	Skytrain
→——	Direction Markers	▭	Parks
———	Main Roads	▨	Golf Courses
———	Secondary Roads	Special	Special Feature
———	Gravel Roads	Option 1	Special Notes
- - - - -	Other Existing Bike Routes	▬▬▬	Highways
= = =	Tunnels	❀	True North
+—+—+	Railways	L___J 1 km	Scale (Approximate)
⌒⌒	Stream or River		
▨▨▨	Water	- - - -	Trails

The information summary lets you know what makes each route special; how physically demanding it is; what kind of road, terrain, and traffic conditions to expect; the type of bike required; how to get to the starting point; and which other routes it connects with. Distances are measured to the nearest 0.1 km (100 m). Elevation gain (Elev Gain) is the estimated total cumulative climb, rounded up to the next 25 m increment. Most routes bring you back to your start, but a few are one way only.

Difficulty is divided into fitness and traffic components.

F • (fitness rating) is a relative overall assessment of physical challenge based on length, and more heavily on cumulative elevation gain, steepness of hills, and surface quality (1 = short and flat, 5 = long and/or with significant elevation gain and/or steep hills and/or rough surface).

T • (traffic hazard factor) is a subjective relative judgement based on traffic density, traffic speed, and road width (1 = no or little traffic, 5 = challenging/ annoying sections). It is weighted heavily towards the worst parts of the route; for example, although a route might be rated T5 overall, much of it might be fairly car-free. Actual traffic conditions will vary with time of day, day of the week, weather, and season.

The main function of the road log is to let you know where to turn and where to find points of interest mentioned in the text. It also provides more information on highlights (opening times (if any), admission fee (approximate 1991 adult fare— most have reduced rates for seniors, children, and families, and may offer memberships), phone number, etc.), hazard warnings, and other tidbits. All times and fees are subject to change and are printed for general guidance only.

Some roads have multiple names, e.g., Highway 7/Loughheed Highway. In Delta in particular, where the first name is a number (as in the case of 64th Street/ Goudy Road) the second name may no longer be in common use. In this case it has been included for historical interest only. Look for the numbers on the road signs and the names on "pioneer markers."

The phrase "at your own risk" is used to describe unofficial railway crossings and other portions of routes (e.g., disused roads or bridges that, although believed generally safe for cycling, may have fallen into a state of disrepair) that may pose hazards to the unwary. Any routes for which a mountain bike is recommended automatically include this caution.

(Route XX) is a note given at the first point where another route crosses, nears, or overlaps the one being described. As well as offering detours, these references also often point to details about the route being described. Additional sources of information are given at the end of the other material.

GVRD parks are generally open from 8 am to dusk (9 pm in summer). Other parks have similar hours. Bicycle riding within parks is not generally permitted except where specified and is sometimes expressly forbidden.

Finally, the detailed description tells you more about the character and setting of the route, and about specific highlights. Sidebars reveal historical details or other interesting information.

For police or ambulance service throughout the area covered by the book, dial 9-1-1.

HOW FAST IS A BIKE, ANYWAY?
(or Why There Aren't Any Suggested Times Given)

"How long will these routes take me?" you might reasonably ask. Well, it all depends on your bike, the road conditions, the traffic, the terrain, the wind, break length, how much weight you're carrying, your fitness, your mood, and your intentions. Go slower than about 5 km/h and you'll have trouble staying up; at the other end of the scale, elite road racers average about 40 km/h over 200 km, while track racers can maintain nearly 60 km/h over 1 km.

If you're a typical recreational rider, you'll probably find that keeping a mountain bike moving above 30 km/h (2 min/km) on good flat roads is hard work and you won't see much besides. With rolling hills and occasional stop signs, make that 24 km/h (2.5 min/km). A moderate pace with a few short pauses here and there might yield 15-20 km/h (3-4 min/km). If you're pretty casual or really get involved in the scenery, expect maybe 10 km/h (6 min/km) or less. On a skinny tired road bike you can expect to go a bit faster for the same effort. Lunch breaks, berry gathering, bird watching, swimming, museum visits, and repairs all count extra, of course. Gravel, head winds, fatigue, dehydration, and low blood sugar can also slow you dramatically.

As an example, consider a 30 km route with good riding conditions. At a relaxed pace, taking two 20-minute breaks and an hour for lunch, the trip could last four hours and 40 minutes (6.4 km/h); a fast racer might cover the same distance in closer to 43 minutes (42 km/h).

WHAT, NO ODOMETER?

Even without an odometer on your bike you can often still determine approximate distance: e.g., using street or house numbers.

Vancouver's north-south address numbering has its zero line along Dundas St, sixteen streets (they should really be avenues) north of 1st Ave. Thus though address hundred-blocks increase southwards along with the avenues, they are out of step by sixteen blocks. Alignment is in some cases poor, so the avenues don't always fall right on the mark. There is about 0.10 km between avenues. Therefore, 1 km is nearly ten blocks or a difference of about 1000 in house numbers, say between 4th Ave and 14th Ave (numbers 2000 and 3000). To calculate the north-south distance between two addresses, subtract them, multiply by the number of kilometres in a block, and divide by the number of addresses in a block. For example, between 555 Main St and 3675 Main St, it's about (3675 - 555) x 0.10 / 100 = 3.1 km.

East-west addresses are measured from Ontario/Carrall St. Distance calculations will likely be less exact than for north-south because although hundred-blocks are typically 0.16 km long, they reach a high of 0.23 km in Point Grey. A kilometre is consequently usually just over six blocks, a bit over four in Point Grey. Calculate distances as for north-south.

You'll need to be a little more industrious to reckon distance this way on angled roads, and don't even think of trying to use this trick in Shaughnessy! Note that the whole downtown peninsula is numbered as if it *weren't* tilted at an angle to the rest.

Burnaby continues Vancouver's numbering system for houses (though not for avenues), but more roads are at angles to the grid.

Richmond's No. 1 Road, No. 2 Road, etc. layout is based on a 1.6 km (one mile) grid, with other major roads filling in the gaps to give a standard 0.8 km block between arterials, and similar spacing for east-west roads. House numbers are 1000 to the arterial block, or 1250 to the kilometre. The zero-zero point? Out in Georgia Strait, a little northwest of the airport.

New Westminster, North Vancouver, West Vancouver, etc. each use their own non-integrated numbering systems! You are invited to calculate the figures for these if you so desire.

Note that even-numbered addresses are found on the south and east sides while odd ones are on the north and west.

Another way to calculate distance is to base it on your speed and time taken, or you could derive it from your cadence, wheel diameter, and gear ratio.

Metric Equivalents	
1 metre (m)	3.3 feet
1 kilometre (km)	5/8 mile
1 litre (L)	7/8 Imperial quart (or 1 US quart)
1 hectare (ha)	2.5 acres
1 kilogram (kg)	2.2 pounds

VANCOUVER, BURNABY & NEW WESTMINSTER

Within Vancouver, Burnaby, and New Westminster, you'll discover not only urban amenities, but also historical richness and a surprising number of parks and scenic places. The terrain ranges from flat to rolling hills, with some steep slopes in north Burnaby.

This map shows you the approximate scope and location of each route; each is numbered somewhere along its length. (To aid readability, higher-numbered routes are broken where they cross lower-numbered ones.) A few roads are labelled to help with access.

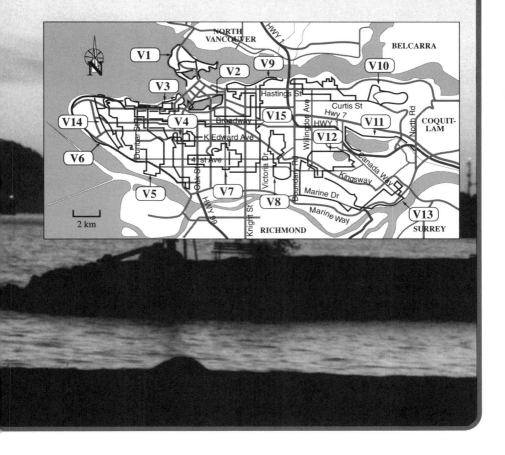

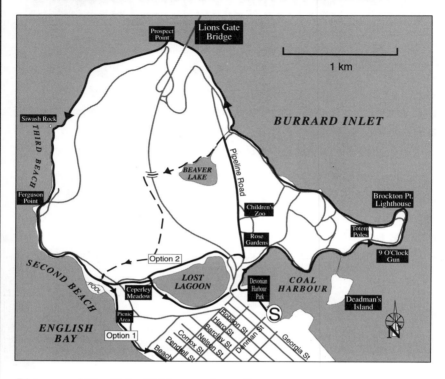

Distance and Elev Gain 10.1 km + options, nil, return

Terrain, Road, Traffic near-level with several short inclines; paved (and firm gravel for Option I); car-free, one-directional bicycle path (and low to moderately busy roads for Option I or II)

Difficulty F1 T1

Bike any bike

Access take Robson Street or other road to West End and turn right on Denman St (Routes V2, V3)

Short Description a seaside ride around Vancouver's favourite park, with options to ride through it or continue along the shoreline

ROAD LOG

Notes: the Seawall Promenade is one-way; **watch for pedestrians and overtaking cyclists; watch for drain gratings**. Only designated cycling paths and roads are used in this route.

0.0 Devonian Harbour Park, N foot of Denman St; head W

0.3 right to follow seawall

0.6 Vancouver Rowing Club

1.3 Royal Van. Yacht Club

1.6 Deadman's Island on right

1.8 totems across to left

2.0 statue of Harry Jerome, runner of the century 1871-1971

2.1 Nine O'Clock Gun on right

2.5 Brockton Point Lighthouse; fountain at top of stairs

2.7 monument to Chehalis shipwreck of 1906

3.3 *Girl in Wetsuit*, 1972, on right; *Empress of Japan* figurehead replica, 1960 (original at Vancouver Maritime Museum)

3.6 Variety Kids' Water Park; Lumbermen's Arch on left; washrooms

4.7 veer left uphill

4.9 keep right to go down wooden bridge; **Caution: *slippery when wet***

5.0 rejoin seawall; cyclists raised above pedestrians

5.1 Lions Gate Bridge, 1938

5.2 Prospect Point Lighthouse

6.6 Siwash Rock; plaque on left commemorates work of James Cunningham

6.9 Third Beach begins

7.1 access to concession, tall trees, Pauline Johnson memorial, Ferguson Point   Teahouse

8.2 veer left up bank, follow parking lot edge

8.5 left around back of Second Beach concession and pool

8.6 left towards Lost Lagoon; or else Option I

8.7 cross road into Ceperley Meadow

8.9 right over bridge; or else Option II

9.1 rhododendron gardens

9.3 left along Lost Lagoon

9.6 washrooms, bus loop, concession; through tunnel

9.8 right at red brick terrace to return to start

10.1 finished

Native totems are sometimes more beautiful unpainted.

Option I: Sunset Beach

8.6 keep straight along shore

8.8 playground, picnic area, washrooms on left

9.3 Lord Stanley statue on left; right on road

9.6 1919 Beach: bizarre concrete stumps

10.0 Joe Fortes memorial fountain and Alexandra Bandshell on left; washrooms and first aid on right at English Bay Beach

10.1 sharp right downhill on path

10.2 sharp left along shore; Inukshuk on point

10.9 Sunset Beach concession and washrooms (Routes V2, V3)

Option II: Beaver Lake Loop

8.9 left to Lost Lagoon Dr., right on road

9.7 left under highway

9.8 left on Pipeline Rd

9.9 rose gardens

10.0 access to children's zoo and train on right

10.7 Tall Trees Grove on right

10.8 left on gravel trail ("Service Vehicles Only") instead of curving right

11.0 Beaver Lake; go right

11.3 bear right at fork to cross small bridge

11.4 cross trail, angle slightly right

11.5 paved, take overpass

11.7 first left turn, gravel

12.2 straight at intersection, then note Seven Sisters site on left

12.4 straight at intersection (with covered bench, fire hydrant)

12.9 either straight to cross road and rejoin main route at 13.0 km (8.5 km mark), or left on paved path to cross road and complete loop at 13.6 km

More information: *Hiking Guide to the Big Trees* by Randy Stoltmann

---

People have been cycling around Stanley Park almost since it opened in 1888. The park's first traffic count, on Sunday, July 23, 1905, revealed "5264 pedestrians, 16 saddle horses, 148 teams, 35 hacks, 176 bicycles and 176 autos." (*Vancouver Sun*, July 4, 1961) They weren't using the seawall, though, for it would be 11 years before the first stones were laid, and the promenade wouldn't be complete for 70 years. The park's popularity has since increased dramatically, ensuring that Sunday afternoon is not the best time for unobstructed cycling.

The route begins by passing interesting and numerous ships, followed by striking views of Vancouver's dramatic skyline. Deadman's Island, now the site of the naval training base HMCS *Discovery*, was long known to the Squamish people as "The Island of Dead Men." In explaining the name, poet Pauline Johnson relates the tale of the gruelling, months-long battle between the tribes of the North and the South. At its climax, a prolonged siege of the island was finally resolved when 200 gallant warriors from the North gave their lives in exchange for the safety of their captured elders, women, and children. The morning after being drenched in the blood of these valiant men, the soil produced flaming fire-flowers. Struck with overpowering terror, the Southerners fled, and peace came once more to the region.

Across the road from Hallelujah Point, named to commemorate the Salvation Army's meetings here, is a group of fine totem poles whose lure no tourist can resist. The petroglyphs on the adjacent rock receive less attention, though. For a time it was the duty of the Brockton Point Lighthouse keeper to fire the nearby Nine O'Clock Gun. Originally fired at 6 pm, to warn fishers of Sunday fishing closures, it now serves only to announce that 9 pm has arrived. In quieter days, its report could sometimes be heard as far upriver as Mission.

On the other side of Brockton Point, the mountains and waterfront industry of the North Shore come into view. Interestingly, Brockton Oval was originally constructed as a cycling track. Inland from the water park, formerly a pool, Lumbermen's Arch stands in tribute to BC's lumber industry. In the 19th century, this open area was the site of Khwaykhway ("Masks"), a Squamish Indian village. There were more villages on the peninsula, including that of the Squamish Chief Khahtsahlano at Chaythoos (Prospect Point), and others from more ancient times. Early road crews encountering shells in old village middens used them as a surfacing material.

Tall Trees Grove, just past Lumberman's Arch, holds several of Stanley Park's surviving Douglas fir monarchs. Although they range to over 70 m in height, they would seem small compared to another park Douglas fir that grew to 99 m — making it even taller than the tallest known tree in all of Canada today, the 95 m Carmanah Giant — when it fell in 1926. Even when dead, these tall trees continue to provide essential perches for raptorial birds such as eagles.

The seawall offers superb views of Deadman's Island and Vancouver skyline.

There is a change in the terrain. Rocky bluffs begin to appear, rising at times over 60 m, sometimes lushly moist and mossy, or overhung at improbable angles with trees desperate for light. One memorable section of cliff at Prospect Point emits a fishy odour, revealing a nesting colony of pelagic cormorants.

Siwash Rock, standing proudly apart, is said (according to one account) to be a young chief on whom the Four Men of the Sagalie Tyee (God) conferred immortality as a monument to his exemplary display of "clean fatherhood" in diligently swimming before the birth of his first child, to give it the best possible start in life. A less-endearing legend says that it is a young man turned to stone as punishment for hunting seals without permission from his chief.

Soon after, you reach the first of several agreeable beaches — Third Beach. Just to your left is Canada's largest known red alder; Canada's largest known maple and an exceptional red cedar are a few minutes' walk inland. High above Third Beach is elegant Ferguson Point Teahouse. Nearby is a monument to Pauline Johnson, who was especially fond of the park. She is credited with coining the name "Lost Lagoon"; it was once part of Coal Harbour so as the tides shifted, she would find her favourite canoeing waters periodically lost to her.

The last part of this route passes this now-enclosed body of water, rhododendron gardens, and squirrel territory. As an option, you can head past the fragrant rose gardens to Beaver Lake, come back through the woods past the stumps of the Seven Sisters; or you could continue towards Sunset Beach, passing the Joe Fortes memorial fountain and the unusual Inukshuk sculpture.

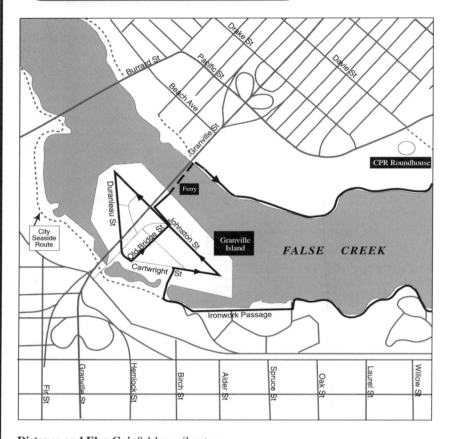

Distance and Elev Gain 8.1 km, nil, return

Terrain, Road, Traffic flat; 5 km on paved bicycle paths, the rest on roads; on Granville Island traffic is busy but slow

Difficulty F1 T3

Bike any bike that can be lifted through the ferry doorway

Access Take Quebec St S from Pacific Blvd or Union St and turn right into the parking lot (Routes V1, V3)

Short Description an easy ride along False Creek that takes in that magnet for amateur scientists of all ages, Science World; the artistic, marine, and gustatory bustle of Granville Island; and a ride on a tiny ferry

ROAD LOG

Caution: *watch for pedestrians and other cyclists and be prepared to slow down or take evasive action*

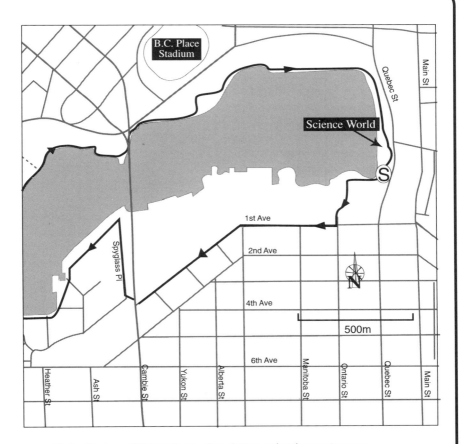

Note: Portions of this route are changing as redevelopment occurs.

0.0 just S of Science World (1455 Quebec St at Terminal Ave.) at the tall, glass-roofed blue shelter; head W along water on Seaside Rte; Science World: $7 (exhibits only) or $11 (with Omnimax), Sun-Fri 10 am-5 pm, Sat 10 am-9 pm (rec. msg.: 687-7832, Omnimax: 875-6664)

0.1 left on gravel (soon paved), then merge onto Ontario St

0.3 right on W 1st Ave; **Caution: _paved shoulder is uneven, gravelly, and obstructed by poles_**

1.1 jog right at tracks (filled in) to go under Cambie Bridge, then right on Spyglass Pl.

1.4 left on red paving blocks along water; note: keep right along the shoreline unless otherwise indicated

1.8 left at Stamps Landing at Monk McQueen's then right to continue along Millbank

2.3 park with small lookout hill and duck pond

2.7 left, then right on Ironwork Passage at marina

2.9 pass end of Granville Is.

3.3 right to Granville Is. at Birch Walk, over small bridge, right again (Route V3)

3.4 left between False Ck Community Ctre and tennis court; water fountain
    Caution: *lots of railway tracks on Granville Island*
3.5 right on Cartwright St
3.6 1241 on left: Inuit Sculpture Exhibition, free, Tue-Sun 10:30 am-4:30 pm (open daily in
    summer) (669-5223); turn abruptly left on Johnson St (straight ahead for hotel and hill)
3.7 1399 on right: Emily Carr College of Art and Design
3.9 Creek House, etc. on right; info centre on left (666-5784)
4.0 Netloft on left
4.1 left on Duranleau St.; Blackberry Books, Netloft on left; kayak shops and other
    marine businesses on right
4.2 bear left on Cartwright St
4.3 Kids Only Market on right, Tue-Sun 10 am-6 pm; Granville Is. Brewery on left
4.4 left on Old Bridge St
4.5 left on Johnston St
4.6 Aquabus ferry: right between Arts Club Theatre (687-1644) and Public Market,
    ramp to dock, 7:30 am-9 pm, $1.25, can only take a few bikes at the time
    (874-9930); get off directly opposite, go right then left on L-shaped dock, up ramp
    and through gate; head left to go under bridge, then right (Route V1)
4.9 right on Seaside Route (gate open dawn to dusk)
* **5.1, 5.4, 5.8** bypass bench areas
6.1 CPR roundhouse and access to Davie St on left
6.5 under Cambie Bridge
6.9 enter Plaza of Nations: BC Place dome beyond to left, fountain on right, Unicorn
    Pub on left
7.0 right at flagpoles, left at big green glass building, then right just beyond and left on
    blacktop along water (gate open dawn to dusk)
7.7 right through parking lot
7.9 keep right on road to loop in front of Science World, then out again; turn sharp
    right on path just before next parking lot
8.1 back at start

Did you ever wonder what it would look like if you could leave your shadow behind? At Science World you can do just that. A wonderful assortment of hands-on exhibits lets you tease yourself with visual illusions, and perform experiments with light, sound, and fluids. Parents can accompany their children through the Search Gallery to discover more about BC's natural history. Live shows and temporary exhibitions add excitement, while up top, in the Omnimax "golf ball," larger-than-life film action unfolds around you on the world's largest domed screen. There are even inexpensive storage lockers to guard your gear while you wander about. The only sour note in the complex — which will hopefully soon change — is the reliance on single-use cups and utensils in the cafeteria.

    Leaving Science World, you follow the city's Seaside Bicycle Route first through a remnant industrial area, then along the water on a bicycle/pedestrian promenade surfaced with several kinds of paving stones. A diversity of housing styles and a park with a pond cover the left while looking right gives views of maritime activities and the dramatic downtown skyline. Granville Island, with all its spirited activity, soon appears.

With more than 260 businesses, studios, and other facilities set within its original industrial framework, Granville Island has something for almost everyone. Children will be delighted with the range of offerings, from puppets to microscopes, at Kids Only Market. Nautically-minded adults will find watercraft from kayaks to yachts, and lovers of theatre needn't go away unfulfilled either.

The art lover can drop by the Emily Carr College of Art & Design (student artwork always seems to be on display) and the Inuit Sculpture Exhibition, with its rotating collection of exquisite works in soapstone, whalebone, and argillite. As well, small art and craft workshops are hidden away everywhere; try in and around the Creek House and the Netloft for gifts. If hunger gnaws, visit the enormous public market or choose from over half a dozen restaurants,

Students' bikes create an impromptu sculpture outside Emily Carr College.

including cooperatively-owned Isadora's. Finally, for some plain old relaxation, climb the hill at the east end and lie down on the grass.

When you're ready to move on, take the colourful little Aquabus across False Creek. Continue on the far shore, past the white-domed BC Place Stadium and the Plaza of Nations, legacies of Expo '86, and the new developments springing up where the rest of this international transportation fair stood, to return to Science World.

Someone who last knew False Creek just 150 years ago would scarcely recognize it at all today. In those days, trout darted to and fro in its tributaries and dense coastal Douglas fir forest reached down to its marshy shores. At high tide, False Creek stretched around to the northeast, creating a temporary island of what is now the downtown peninsula.

As the town of Granville, later to be Vancouver, began to develop on the shore of Burrard Inlet, loggers came in the 1870s to cut the trees. In 1886, after extorting huge land grants covering a quarter of modern-day Vancouver, including much of False Creek, the CPR agreed to extend its rails west from Port Moody. In the following years, the CPR built its yards — only the roundhouse survived Expo '86 — on the north shore of False Creek, confirming the area's industrial tone.

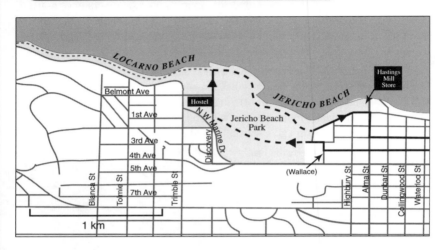

Distance and Elev Gain 13.6 km, 75 m, return

Terrain, Road, Traffic largely gentle hills; paved except 2.8 km on good gravel trails; mostly on quiet streets with about 0.6 km moderate traffic, one espesially tough crossing

Difficulty F2 T3

Bike any bike

Access from downtown, take Burrard Bridge, then right on Chestnut St and right on Whyte Ave; from W 4th Ave or Cornwall Ave, take Cypress St N to Whyte and turn right; bike only: from city's Seaside Route on S side of False Ck, take first road SW after Burrard Bridge (Routes V2, V5, V6)

Short Description much more than a trip to the beach

ROAD LOG

0.0 in front of big crab at H.R. MacMillan Planetarium, 1100 Chestnut St, Vanier Pk; head W; Vancouver Museum, $5 ($8 with Maritime Museum), Tue-Sun/Hol 10 am-5 pm (Jun-Sep: every day 'til 9 pm) (736-7736); H.R. MacMillan Planetarium, astronomy shows $5, laser-rock shows $7 (736-3656)

0.1 right on Chestnut St

0.2 left on Ogden Ave (follow bike route markers)

0.3 Maritime Museum in Hadden Pk on right, behind 30 m totem pole (1958, design: Chief Martin, Kwakiutl), $4, daily 10 am-5 pm (737-2212)

0.5 curve left on Maple St

0.6 right on McNicoll Ave; Kitsilano Beach Pk on right; curve onto Arbutus St

1.0 right through parking lot just past tennis court; left just beyond its end on paved path; right just before Cornwall Ave

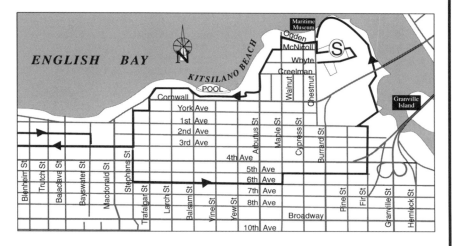

- **1.4** washrooms on right just past Vine, Kits Showboat and pool behind
- **1.6** right on Pt Grey Rd
- **2.0** curve left onto Trafalgar St; little park on right with stairs to rocky shoreline
- **2.1** cross Cornwall St; signal push button within reach of cyclists
- **2.2** right on York Ave
- **2.3** left on Stephens St; fine Craftsman homes from 1910-12
- **2.6** right on W 3rd Ave
- **2.8** Tatlow Pk on right, washrooms
- **3.0** row of near identical Craftsman homes on left (Routes V5, V6)
- **4.4** right on Wallace St
- **4.5** left on W 2nd Ave
- **4.6** straight on gravel path into Jericho Pk beyond parking lot
- **4.8** keep left at fork
- **5.1** keep straight through blackberry country
- **5.4** right on Discovery St (curb)
- **5.5** 1515 on left: Canadian Hostelling Association
- **5.7** bear left, hugging E edge of parking lot at E end of Locarno Beach, then straight N on gravel; rest rooms on left
- **5.8** right on city's Seaside Route to pass Jericho Sailing Centre
- **6.2** follow edge of large plaza area
- **6.4** keep left at fork to follow beach
- **6.7** bear right on main trail, then keep left at fork
- **6.9** join Pt Grey Rd eastbound
- **7.0** 3875 on left: *Brock House,* 1912-3, English Arts and Crafts style

Be courteous when cyclists and pedestrians must share the same route.

7.2	Royal Vancouver Yacht Club on left
7.4	right on Alma St (busier); detour left for Hastings Mill Store at 1575, Sat-Sun, 1-4 pm
7.6	left on W 2nd
8.6	right on Bayswater St
8.7	left on W 3rd
9.0	right on Stephens St
9.1	cross W 4th Ave **(use care)**; W beyond parking lot is the Naam, a Vancouver vegetarian tradition, 24 hrs
9.3	left on W 6th Ave; maples form a tunnel of green
10.3	cross Arbutus St., on SE corner is the Arbutus Grocery, 1908
10.5	left on Maple St; 2150 on right: SPEC (736-7732), City Farmer (736-2250), etc.
10.6	right on W 5th Ave
10.9	cross Burrard St (challenging)
11.2	1637 on left: Que Pasa tortilla factory (sorry, no tours)
11.2	left on Fir St
11.4	cross W 4th Ave **(careful of turning traffic)**
11.5	straight, then curve left
11.7	right on W 1st Ave
11.8	left on Creekside Dr.
12.0	right on paver/paved bicycle/pedestrian path at road end **(caution)**

A dense forest, supporting at least seven trout- and salmon-bearing streams, once covered the south shore of English Bay. The mighty cedars that grew here were used by the native peoples for constructing their great canoes. Loggers came to the eastern part of present-day Kitsilano in the 1870s, and settlers began to trickle in. During the 1890s, fashionable West-Enders would row across the mouth of False Creek or cycle over the new Granville Street Bridge to spend the day — or camp for the summer — at what was then called Greer's Beach.

12.2	pass under Burrard Bridge
12.3	right at stop sign, then left on gravel along shore
12.9	*The Gate to a Northwest Passage*, on left, by Chung Hung, is a memorial to Capt. George Vancouver
13.0	bear left; right for Heritage Harbour (736-4431)
13.1	left on Chestnut St
13.3	left on Whyte Ave
13.5	left past Gordon MacMillan Southam Observatory (on right) free viewing on clear weekends, call ahead (738-2855)
13.6	back at the crab

This trip begins at the home of the biggest crab in Vancouver: the one by sculptor George Norris that stands riveted in front of the H.R. MacMillan Planetarium and Vancouver Museum. The Vancouver Museum provides fascinating insights into the lives of the early peoples of the Fraser delta and the techniques used by archaeologists to unravel the lost secrets of ages past. An excellent collection of more recent native handicrafts and cultural items includes the finest of basketry and amazing masks, such as those of Bookwus, the Kwakiutl wild man of the woods who seeks to imprison the spirits of the drowned in the unreal forest world by persuading them to share his ghost food.

The star shows featured at the H.R. MacMillan Planetarium will take you to even more-distant times and far-away places, and there are exciting laser-rock spectacles as well.

The nearby Maritime Museum maintains on permanent display the fanciful *Empress of Japan* figurehead and an exhibit profiling the ships that call at Vancouver. For some humour, check out the 1915 painting *Landing of Captain Vancouver*. The RCMP *St Roch*, however, is definitely the highlight. This was the first ship to navigate the frigid Northwest Passage from west to east (from 1940-42, and back again in 1944) and the first to circumnavigate North America. She is remarkably well preserved and restored, bearing on her deck and in her hold many items associated with these historic Arctic voyages.

The bicycle is an ideal second vehicle for the sailor.

Follow the lovely Kitsilano Beach shoreline, and make your way past many of the area's original 1910s Craftsman bungalows en route to Jericho Park. Since the days when Jeremiah Rogers ran a logging show here, Jerry's Cove — now shortened to Jericho — has become (since 1973) a beautiful beachfront park, with grassy picnic areas and duck ponds, and is the site of the annual Folk Music Festival. Like Stanley Park, it too served time as a military reserve.

After a swim or a laze on the beach, head back past the relocated 1865 Hastings Mill store, the oldest surviving building in the city. Continue back east, pausing at the Society Promoting Environmental Conservation (SPEC) building, where you'll find not only the offices of this and several other environmental groups, but also the wondrous Ability Garden cultivated here by City Farmer. As well as a wide range of succulent vegetables and pretty flowers, you'll find an informative demonstration of composting techniques.

Back at the Seaside Route, follow it beneath the Burrard Bridge and around the large grassy area behind the planetarium. Here you will often see kite-flyers, and, behind the Maritime Museum, wooden sailing vessels, a native canoe, and other interesting craft at Heritage Harbour.

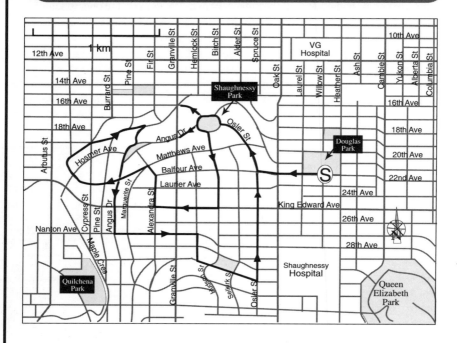

Distance and Elev Gain   8.9 km, 100 m, return

Terrain, Road, Traffic   gently rolling; paved; secondary residential streets with 0.5 km on busier King Edward Ave

Difficulty   F2 T3

Bike   if it's in style, use it

Access   take Heather St (13 blocks W of Cambie St) to 22nd Ave and go one block W (Route 6)

Short Description   a sampling of some of Vancouver's finest heritage homes on their beautifully treed, curving streets

ROAD LOG

0.0   801 W 22nd Ave, Douglas Pk Community Centre; head W

0.3   cross Oak St to enter Shaughnessy on Balfour Ave

0.4   1063 on right: two large monkey puzzles (*Araucaria* or Chile Pine)

0.5   right on Osler St

0.8   3498 on right: *Iowa*, 1913-14, Gothic Revival and others, built for Frank L. Buckley, lumberman/industrialist

1.0   right on The Crescent around Shaughnessy Pk, focal point of Shaughnessy

1.3   detour right on McRae Ave to see 1489 on right: *Hycroft*, 1909-12, Second Renaissance Revival, built for Alexander Duncan McRae, timber/coal/fisheries/real estate baron and later senator; turn back

1.4 1402 on right: *Nichol House*, 1912-13, English Arts and Crafts, built for Walter Cameron Nichol, prominent newspaperman and later Lt Gov.

1.5 right on The Crescent

1.6 right on Angus Dr.

1.7 1499 on right: unknown, 1914, Spanish Colonial Revival; **turn around** at Granville St to go back along other side of Angus Dr.

1.9 right on The Crescent

2.0 right on Hudson St

2.6 right on King Edward Ave

3.0 cross Granville St

3.2 right on Alexandra St

3.4 bear left at Balfour Ave to stay on Alexandra St

3.5 left on Matthews Ave

3.6 1690 Marguerite on left: *Glen Brae*, 1910-11, built for William Lamont Tait, lumber and real estate magnate; keep right on Matthews Ave

3.7 3802 Angus on left: *Hendry House*, 1911, Tudor Revival (recently refurbished), built for J.E. Tucker (lumberman) and sold to John Hendry, prominent lumber mogul

4.2 Matthews Ave curves onto Cedar Cr. at Maple Cr. (Route V6)

4.3 bear right past Maple St

4.5 straight, then bear right onto 19th Ave at Cypress St

4.6 3490 Cedar Cr. on left: name unknown, c. 1914, Tudor Revival, impressive stone-faced home

4.7 curve left at Pine Cr.

4.9 keep right to pass Pine St

5.0 sharp right on Marpole Ave

5.2 right on Angus Dr. at Angus Pk

5.8 cross King Edward Ave into Second Shaughnessy; 1808 W King Edward Ave on right: *A.B. Weeks House*, 1923, Mission Style

6.0 left on Nanton Ave

6.5 cross Granville St; 1490 on right: St John's "Shaughnessy" Memorial Church, 1949

6.7 right on Cartier St

6.9 left on Connaught Dr. to pass Devonshire Pk

7.4 left on Osler St

8.0 cross King Edward Ave back into First Shaughnessy

8.4 right on Balfour Ave

8.9 back at Douglas Pk

More information: *Exploring Vancouver 2*, by Harold Kalman , *Vancouver Heritage Inventory*, Summary Report, phase II, by Allen Parker and Associates

Towering Chilean Araucaria *(monkey puzzles) grace several Shaughnessy mansions.*

When the formerly upper-class West End began to attract commoners, the wealthy thought it had become too busy. The CPR (which had engineered not only the rails leading west but also a generous land grant for itself) was ready, as it had been with its West End properties when the East End became crowded.

Hendry House, *recently refurbished, is ready for another 80 years.*

Shaughnessy Heights, which opened in 1909, was for over two decades the exclusive province of the well-to-do. First Shaughnessy (bounded north-south by West 16th and King Edward avenues and east-west by Arbutus and Oak streets), with its somewhat whimsically laid-out streets, was designed with generous lots. These were gratefully purchased by Vancouver's social elite, who called upon the foremost architects of the day to build their mansions. Even though it's no longer exclusively a neighbourhood of single-family homes, thanks to building restrictions Shaughnessy retains an aura of gentility and a park-like ambience.

Before setting forth, pause a moment to admire the giant weeping willows at the northeast corner of Douglas Park; they're among the finest in the Lower Mainland. Then, once you cross Oak Street onto Balfour Avenue, the change is abrupt; you know you're in Shaughnessy. Here the timber barons, captains of industry, and other wealthy beings could retire to their lavish homes and gentle, treed streets to socialize after a hard day.

The street and yard trees, which have matured beautifully, complement some of the finest homes of their styles anywhere in Greater Vancouver. In Shaughnessy you'll find outstanding houses in many traditions, including English Arts and Crafts, Mission Revival, Craftsman, Colonial Revival, Georgian Revival, and even Queen Anne. One of the earliest and finest is *Glen Brae*, completed in 1911 for Scottish-born timber and real estate magnate William Tait. A near-palatial structure, it must have appeared even more magnificent when its exquisite Scottish-made wrought iron fence was still gilded. For a time the house also fell into infamy when it briefly became the Canadian headquarters of the Ku Klux Klan.

This trip takes you into Second Shaughnessy as well. Although its larger-than-average lots and houses mark it, too, as more a neighbourhood for blue blood than for blue collars, it never did achieve the level of distinction reached by its older sibling to the north.

RIGHT: Without the exquisite wrought-iron fence, Glen Brae *would be just another Shaughnessy mansion.*

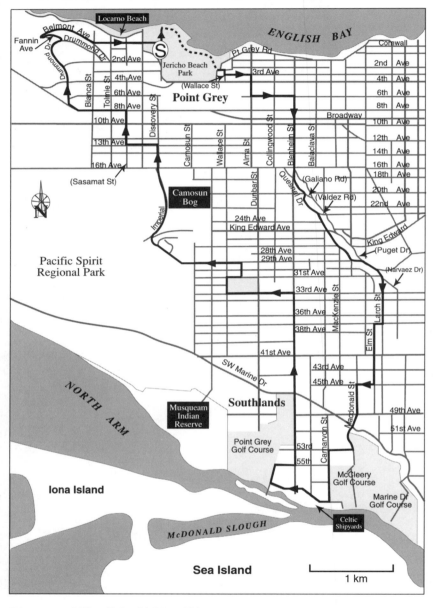

Distance and Elev Gain 22.7 km, 200 m, return

Terrain, Road, Traffic flat, with two each prolonged descents and ascents (steep in places); good pavement, some slightly rough spots, with 1.3 km of good unpaved trail; traffic mostly light, occasionally moderate

Difficulty F4 T3

Bike gears and good brakes recommended

Access from W 4th Ave. turn N on NW Marine Drive, then right again 0.3 km later on Discovery St; or, bike only: from city's Seaside Route, begin at Alma, the 2.0 km mark (Routes V3, V6, V14, V15)

Short Description a shore-to-shore ride across Vancouver, with lots of street trees, to visit a patch of country within the city and a shipyard, returning past an outstanding Gothic Revival former convent and BC's oldest bog in its urban forest park setting

ROAD LOG

0.0 1515 Discovery St: Canadian Hostelling Association (224-7111); head N

0.2 bear left along E edge of Locarno Beach parking lot; continue straight N on gravel trail; rest rooms on left

0.3 right on Seaside Rte

0.4 past Jericho Sailing Centre on left

0.7 keep right along large plaza area

0.8 keep left along waterfront; open grassy space on right is site of annual Folk Music Festival; sandy beach

1.2 bear right at fork; follow bike route signs S along parking lot

1.4 left on W 2nd Ave

1.5 right on Wallace St

1.6 left on W 3rd Ave

2.0 right on Alma St (busier) (Route V15)

2.3 left on W 6th Ave

2.6 eagle mural on Bayview Community School

2.9 right on Blenheim St

3.9 cross W 16th Ave (caution); begin climbing

4.1 angle left on Quesnel Dr.

4.4 cross W 20th Ave and Galiano Rd

4.6 cross W 22nd Ave and Valdez Rd

5.0 cross King Edward; **Caution: _divided, poor visibility_**

5.3 angle left across MacKenzie St at W 27th Ave; loose gravel alert

5.6 left on W 29th Ave (downhill)

5.7 right on Puget Dr. (better views)

6.0 bear right at W 31st and Narvaez Dr.

6.3 cross W 33rd Ave onto Larch St

6.7 right on W 37th Ave; 2490, on SE corner: St Mary's Kerrisdale Anglican, 1913

6.8 left on Elm St

Once you start watching seagulls, their antics can entertain for hours.

7.2	cross W 41st Ave (left for Kerrisdale)
7.6	right on W 45th Ave
7.9	left on Macdonald St
8.0	6200 on left: picturesque, ivy-covered house
8.3	cross W 49th Ave; **Caution: *poor visibility***
8.5	cross SW Marine Dr.; **Caution: *poor visibility***
8.8	right on W 53rd Ave; (to dyke: take Macdonald St past Southlands Riding and Polo Club (at 7025, 263-4817), then follow E side of McCleery Golf Course parking lot, continuing on a gravel road; walking W along shore leads to a trail (past blackberries) to Celtic Shipyards
9.1	left on Carnarvon St
9.8	right on Celtic Ave
10.0	3150 on left: Celtic Shipyards
10.7	right on Carrington St
10.9	right on W 55th Ave; enormous home on NE corner
11.2	left on Blenheim St
11.9	begin climbing
13.6	left on W 33rd Ave
14.1	cross Dunbar St;
14.3	Memorial Park W walk-through (washrooms at rear of large brown building)
14.5	right on Wallace St
14.7	right on 31st Ave; **Caution: *tilted road slabs***
14.9	left on Highbury St
15.1	left on W 29th Ave

Some sites are best explored on foot.

15.2	3851 on right: former Convent of the Sacred Heart, Gothic Revival, 1911-12
15.8	cross Camosun St, Pacific Spirit Regional Park on left (GVRD: 224-5739) (Route V14)
16.6	curve right on Imperial Dr.; **caution: *watch for traffic squeeze!***
17.2	Camosun Bog access road on right, BC's biggest heronry on left
17.6	cross W 16th Ave to continue on Discovery St; **Caution: *unsigned intersections ahead***
17.9	left on W 13th Ave
18.4	right on Sasamat St; enormous butternut on left at alley grew from nut planted in 1926
18.9	left on W 8th Ave
19.4	cross Blanca St; 8th becomes a wide, quiet divided boulevard
19.7	right on Drummond Dr., continuing straight on trail, then on pavement again
20.0	cross 4th Ave; **Caution: *fast traffic***
20.7	left on Fannin Ave.
21.0	road curves sharply, becomes Belmont Ave

21.8 Caution: *descend steeply through unsigned intersections with steep descents from right*

22.7 right on Discovery St to finish at hostel

Notes: Mountain bike rentals are available to hostel guests ($18/day).

If detouring into Pacific Spirit Regional Park, please read description for Route V14.

Horses living in Vancouver? Yes — Southlands is undoubtedly the only part of the city where horses even approach outnumbering people on an average workday. This route starts across the Point Grey peninsula from Southlands, at the Vancouver Hostel. Beginning with a jaunt along the beach, you soon tear yourself away and head south.

The street trees and the varied architecture here (and later in the trip, too) are a pleasant contrast to many recent housing developments. Even the older, near-identical developer houses on W 14th Avenue, for example, remind us that we didn't used to need a monster house that occupied the whole lot.

Climbing fairly steeply, then gradually, you soon discover uncommon elevated views of the downtown skyline and the Arbutus valley. Navigation can be a little tricky, but keep on a gentle upgrade and you should be okay. You do eventually descend, however, and then resume climbing again on Puget Dr; here are the best views of all.

Once on the plateau, there is an immediate difference; the street trees tower above, filtering the sun's harsh light. They're mostly tall elms, oaks, birches, and maples, but in springtime the majestic flowering cherries and plums are unrivalled. If you forgot lunch, three or four blocks east is Kerrisdale, a commercial district retaining some of its earlier charm.

Celtic Shipyard helps keep Vancouver's nautical traditions alive.

Descending towards the Fraser River, you'll catch glimpses of the Gulf Islands on the horizon. Beyond Marine Drive is a warning sign bearing the horse-and-rider motif. You have arrived.

In Southlands, the lots are large, horses graze peacefully in the fields, and the curbless roads are cracked and patched. The Southlands Riding and Polo Club, with its big barn, jumping facilities, and bridle path, provides your first opportunity to experience some horsing around. Consider a side trip through the McCleery Golf Course to the Fraser dyke, but watch for flying golf balls. Looking north from here, only the familiar mountains remind you that you're in Vancouver.

Continuing south, you come to a severe looking chain link fence. It encloses the new premises of Celtic (that's *C* as in *cell*) Shipyards, owned by the Musqueam band. It's worth parking your bike and asking at the office if you can walk around and admire the ships in for repairs. (This is a working facility, not a museum, so watch out for moving equipment and only enter the buildings if invited to.)

Convent of the Sacred Heart—one of Vancouver's finest gothic structures.

At the foot of Blenheim Street begins a new seaside walk leading to the new subdivision on recently deforested Deering Island. (Some people thought it would make a great park instead.) Along the route north, the month of June brings the wonderfully fragrant tresses of the black locusts, the creamy snow of their fallen petals thickly carpeting the shoulders of the road.

A climb and slight descent bring you to Memorial Park West, a dandy place for a rest or a picnic. Just beyond is the magnificent gothic former Convent of the Sacred Heart, now a campus of St George's private school.

Pacific Spirit Park provides a prominent nature highlight for this tour. A tribute to the citizens who rallied to have it designated as a park in the late 1980s, it is an extremely popular venue for walking, jogging, mountain biking (Route V14), nature study, and orienteering. At its edge, 2000 year old Camosun Bog, BC's oldest, is a treasure trove of unusual plants. The Greater Vancouver Regional District is now working to reverse the changes suffered by this fragile site since nearby urban development disrupted the water table.

Pause at Sasamat and West 8th Avenue for views of the harbour, then follow 8th as it becomes a grand boulevard with no destination! Cutting to the right, you wind through the domain of the mansion-building set and descend quite steeply back to Jericho Park.

RIGHT: Some older bridges do accommodate cyclists, but only in one direction at a time, if there are no pedestrians.

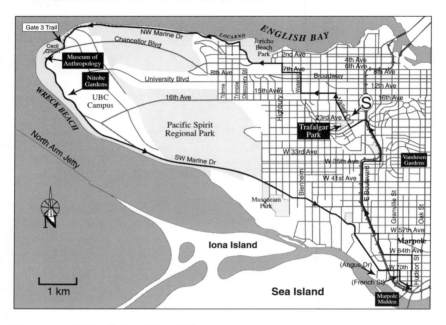

Distance and Elev Gain 31.2 km, 225 m, return

Terrain, Road, Traffic gently rolling except one longer climb and one short but steep one; paved; mostly secondary roads or with paved shoulder or cycling route (11 km), but with occasional short, busier sections

Difficulty F4 T3

Bike any bike good for the distance, gears recommended

Access from W King Edward (c. 25th Ave) at Granville St, head 1.4 km W to Yew St, turn right and then go 0.4 km W on 23rd Ave; or from Macdonald St, head 0.5 km E on W 23rd Ave (Routes V3, V5, V14, V15)

Short Description an off-grid loop passing the popular swimming beaches of Point Grey, the cultural highlights of UBC, the mansions of Southwest Marine Drive, the site of a 2400-year-old native midden, and a likely cycling commuter route.

ROAD LOG

0.0 Valley Dr. at W 23rd Ave, NE corner of Trafalgar Pk; proceed NW

0.7 right on Trafalgar St to cross 16th Ave

0.8 left on W 15th Ave (Route V5)

2.0 right on Waterloo St

2.5 cross W 10th Ave (patience)

2.6	Agora Food Co-op in red building on left just before Broadway (Route V15)
2.8	left on W 7th Ave
3.4	right on Highbury St
3.6	left on W 4th Ave (busier) (Route V3)
4.0	Jericho Pk E on right
4.5	angle right on NW Marine Dr. (city Seaside Route bypass); **Caution**: *occasional parked cars, pedestrians crossing*
5.0	1515 Discovery St on right: CHA Vancouver
5.1	4397 W 2nd Ave on left: handsome *Aberthau*/Pt Grey Community Ctre, 1909-13
5.3	curve right
5.5	curve left; Locarno Beach, washrooms (option to take Seaside Route)
6.2	Spanish Banks, washrooms (Route V14)
7.9	end of city Seaside Route, begin climbing
8.2	entering Pacific Spirit Regional Pk (GVRD: 224-5739)
8.6	entering University Endowment Lands
9.5	commemorative plaque: "The Last Spanish Exploration" on right
9.7	angle right on Chancellor Blvd; Gate 3 Trail to Tower Beach on right
9.8	option: take Cecil Green Pk Rd to end to get behind Museum of Anthropology for Haida house exhibit and totem poles or to watch sunset
10.0	Museum of Anthropology on right, gift shop, go down stairs near end of pkg lot or take service road around from end; $5, Tue-Sun 11 am-5 pm (free and 'til 9 pm on Tue, open Mon in summer) (822-3825)
10.3	Nitobe Memorial Gardens; paved path begins on left opposite Norman MacKenzie House, free mid Oct-mid Mar 10 am-3 pm Mon-Fri, rest of Mar 10-6, Apr-May 10-7, Jun-Aug 10-8, Sept 10-6, Oct 10-5, can continue on path past Place Vanier housing and turn right to join Marine Dr. at Gate 6
10.8	bike racks on right mark Gate 6 Trail to Wreck Beach
11.9	angle right around gate onto old Marine Dr.; or detour straight 0.3 km to UBC Botanical Gardens' Asian Garden, Food Garden, gift shop, etc.; $3.50 (UBC students free), 10 am-6 pm, (free mid Oct-Mar from 11 am); (822-4259)
12.3	beach access
13.1	lookout
13.4	bear right on main Marine Dr.
14.5	lookout, monument to exploration of Fraser River
16.9	pass W 41st Ave, beginning of Musqueam Pk on right
18.4	pass Blenheim St, turnoff to Southlands
19.9	Maple Grove Pk on left
20.7	2170 on right: Spanish Colonial Revival style *Rio Vista*, 1930, belonged to beverage magnate Harry F. Reifel and was featured in Gardens Beautiful tours of the '40s
21.5	1920 on right: Spanish Colonial Revival style *Casa Mia*, 1932, belonged to beverage magnate George C. Reifel and was also on tours
21.8	road curves onto W 70th Ave at Angus St

22.4	cross Granville St (busier)
22.5	right on French St
22.8	angle left on W 73rd Ave; Marpole Pk on left, with Marpole Midden memorial marker at SE corner
23.2	left on Hudson St (few businesses remain in old commercial core of Marpole)
23.7	cross W 70th Ave
24.2	left on W 64th Ave
	Caution: *unsigned intersections ahead*
24.7	cross Granville
25.2	right on E Boulevard
25.6	road curves briefly N to become Angus St
25.9	left on W 57th Ave
26.0	right on E Boulevard
26.6	Victory Gardens begin on left past Maple St
28.1	5350 on right: Pt Grey Sec. School,1928-29
28.2	grand old horse chestnut trees
28.4	curve right on W 35th Ave; short, steep climb with sharp descent
29.0	left on Pine Cres.
29.2	cross W 33rd Ave; Quilchena Pk across tracks to left
30.2	road curves right to become Maple Cres.
30.3	left on divided King Edward Ave (use care)
31.0	right on Valley Dr.
31.2	route completed

The Haida house exhibit may be your best chance to see how the Haida traditionally lived.

It does the spirit good to get off the rectilinear street grid now and then. That's why this route takes in mainly roads that run diagonally or curve back and forth as they wend their way from one place to another. Today's Southwest Marine Drive, for example, is said to follow essentially the same route as it did back in 1863 when Hugh McRoberts and his crew spent just 13 weeks cutting the narrow original North Arm trail the 19 km from New Westminster to the Musqueam Reserve, as a bypass to the sea during winter freeze-up.

Beginning amid the flowering cherries and plums at Trafalgar Park, you make your way out to Jericho Park. From there you pass kilometre after kilometre of beach, although by the time you get to the University of British Columbia (UBC) campus, you're separated from it by 300 m horizontally and 75 m vertically. The isolated section from Tower Beach to Wreck Beach has become known for its "clothing optional" character.

The campus itself is also worth investigating, for the renowned displays of native cultural items at the Museum of Anthropology, the calming and satisfying walking paths at the Nitobe and Botanical Gardens, the architecture of the older science buildings and the newer subterranean Sedgewick Library, and the wealth of information available through the substantial library system. Although UBC was created on paper as BC's first public institution of higher learning in 1908, its relocation from its original 1915 temporary quarters to Point Grey was not realized until 1925, after frustrated students and faculty had staged the "Great Trek of '22" to protest the delay.

Continuing through Pacific Spirit Park, you find your surroundings wooded, with several viewpoints to the south. Then, back in the city, you pass some of its fancier homes, overlooking the Fraser. To the benefit of the many cyclists who use Southwest Marine Drive, city hall has added paved shoulders.

As you continue through Kerrisdale towards the end of the ride, watch for older commercial buildings and the Medieval Gothic Revival style Point Grey Secondary.

Harry Eburne set up his first store in 1881, at the site of the settlement that would for a time bear his name; in 1916, 25 years after he relocated to Sea Island, it would be renamed Marpole to reduce confusion with the other Eburne across the water. Although Harry was one of the early settlers, he had been preceded by the McCleery brothers and their uncle, Hugh McRoberts, and a few others in the mid 1860s.

Long before any of these pioneers arrived, when the mouth of the Fraser was much further inland and salt water lapped at these densely-forested shores, another group of people was moving into the area. They were among the ancestors of today's Coast Salish people, and their use of the site was to span nearly a thousand years, until around 450 AD. Over the following centuries the forest reclaimed the land, growing strong and tall.

When the later newcomers had cleared away the ancient trees, they found an enormous midden (debris heap) covering 1.8 ha. Today most of the evidence of occupation by the earlier native people has been covered over by urban development. However, artifacts recovered during the excavations of the 1890s and early 20th century have led archaeologists to suggest that this long ago era represented a peak of cultural richness never surpassed on this part of the coast.

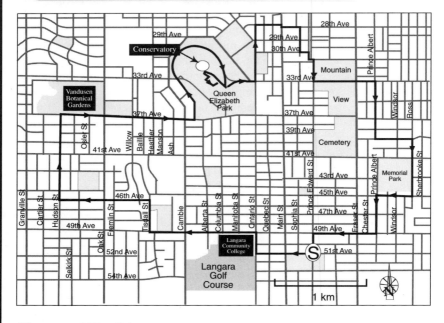

Distance and Elev Gain	14.7 km, 125 m, return
Terrain, Road, Traffic	mostly gentle slopes, with one moderate climb/descent; paved roads; on quieter roads with 2.5 km of moderate traffic streets
Difficulty	F3 T3
Bike	any bike
Access	N on Prince Edward Ave from SE Marine Dr. or S from anywhere S of Kingsway; or take E 51Ave E from Main St or W from Fraser St (Route V15)
Short Description	a ride through the residential areas of central and southeastern Vancouver, featuring beautiful gardens, views, and some unusual buildings

ROAD LOG

0.0   E 51st Ave at Prince Edward St, Sunset Arena; head west

0.1   Sunset Nursery behind hedge on left

0.3   cross Main St; on right: "Little India"

0.6   right on Ontario St; on left: Vancouver Community College Langara Campus

0.8   left on W 49th Ave

2.0   right on Tisdall St

2.2   left on W 46th Ave

3.2   right on Hudson St

4.1 right on W 37th Ave

4.5 entrance to VanDusen Botanical Gardens, $4.25, 10 am-8 pm (winter 4 pm), 266-7194 (take off 0.3 km if you don't go in)

4.8 exit left

5.4 RCMP buildings on left, near Heather St

5.8 cross Cambie St

6.0 left on Kersland Dr.

6.5 turn left, then left again to head N

7.4 keep right at fork

7.6 right towards summit

7.8 keep straight; Seasons Restaurant on right (upscale, 874-8008)

7.9 end of road; walk to viewpoints and Bloedel Conservatory ($2.70, 10 am-9:30 pm (winter, 5 pm), 872-5513); leave to right (on road or walking across plaza) to cross reservoir roof parking lot

8.3 exit left; then head right, keep right

8.9 right on Midlothian Ave

9.0 left on Ontario St; Nat Bailey Stadium on left

9.6 right on E 28th Ave

9.9 right on Main St, then left on E 28th Ave **(use care)**

10.1 right on Sophia St

10.3 left on E 30th Ave

10.4 right on John St

10.5 left on E 31st Ave, then right on Prince Edward St

Pause a moment to reflect upon the lives of Vancouver's pioneers.

10.8 left on E 33rd Ave (busier); Mountain View Cemetery

11.4 right on Prince Albert St; watch for unsigned intersections

12.0 left on E 39th Ave

12.2 960 on right: Sir Alexander Mackenzie School, 1930

12.4 right on Ross St

12.6 cross E 41st Ave; Memorial Pk S on right

13.0 right on E 45th Ave

13.4 left on Prince Albert St

13.9 right on E 49th Ave

14.2 525 on right: Universal Buddhist Temple, 1977

14.5 left on Prince Edward St

14.7 back at start

This isn't exclusively a garden tour, though it does include some of the city's botanical highlights and begins next to Vancouver's Sunset Nursery. Here they grow many of the plants and trees used by the City of Vancouver, in parks and along streets, including 1/4 million bedding plants a year and the tropicals for the Bloedel Conservatory. Just into the trip you pass one end of the two-block stretch of Main Street where you can get everything from dahl to saris: Vancouver's "Little India."

Van Dusen Botanical Gardens will become still more attractive as its trees mature.

Continuing west, you skirt the Langara campus of Vancouver Community College at the corner of Langara Golf Course, which, on those rare occasions when the snow gets too deep for cycling, is patronized by cross-country skiers. Along West 46th Avenue and Hudson Street the lawns and gardens seem especially well manicured. Better still as a place to make or renew your acquaintance with a whole range of our floral friends is VanDusen Botanical Gardens.

Queen Elizabeth Park (once the site of basalt quarrying for street surfacing) also has fine flower gardens, and contains Canada's first civic arboretum. At its centre, the flat summit of Little Mountain supports Vancouver's best-known greenhouse, the dome shaped Bloedel Conservatory, home to plants and birds of more tropical origins. Almost Vancouver's highest point, the adjacent deck is a favourite spot for panoramic views to the north and west (be sure to notice *Photo Session* by J. Seward Johnson, Jr) while the roof of the nearby reservoir (patrolled by a caretaker in a rowboat when it was yet uncovered) gives a better view to the east.

A detour to the north takes you past Nat Bailey Stadium (named to honour Nat Bailey's loyal patronage of baseball during the '50s and '60s), to cross Main Street once again, this time in the vicinity of antique and curio shops.

To be fully appreciated, the next half kilometre should be covered just as dawn breaks on an early spring day, for this is when the magnificent cherry blossoms overhanging Sophia Street are seen to their best advantage. Turning east again, you pass through Mountain View Cemetery, Vancouver's largest, established in 1886. Older plots still have gran-

One day the trees may block this view of the city from Queen Elizabeth Park.

ite borders. On the other side of Fraser Street is Vancouver's only Art Deco school, named after Sir Alexander Mackenzie.

Memorial Park, which you pass shortly afterwards, opened in 1926 as a memorial to soldiers who fought in World War I. Besides a prominent cenotaph, it featured grass tennis courts, a Gyro Club playground, and a 140 yard whippet racing track. The brown field house was added around 1930.

One last point of interest on the route is the exuberantly appointed, dragon-fronted Universal Buddhist Temple on East 49th Avenue.

Have you ever wanted to get lost in a hedge maze, just like they did in England during the 17th and 18th centuries? And remember those wonderful cacti that you saw advertised in magazines when you were a child but when you ordered the seeds, they didn't look quite the same? Ever seen birches so stark white they look painted? These, more rhododendrons and heathers than you knew existed, and other delights await at VanDusen Botanical Display Gardens.

Surprisingly young, the gardens were created in the early 1970s on land formerly occupied by the old Shaughnessy Heights Golf Course (built early in the century by the Vancouver Lawn Bowling Club). The sculptures positioned throughout the site are the offspring of the Vancouver International Stone Sculpture Symposium, held during July and August of 1975, immediately before the gardens opened to the public.

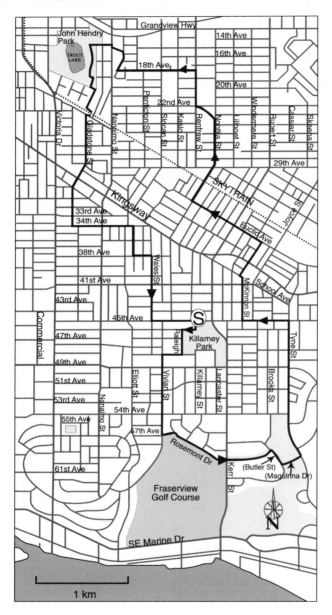

Distance and Elev Gain 14.6 km, 150 m, return

Terrain, Road, Traffic rolling; quieter residential roads except for 0.5 on mostly-paved path; 2.6 km on moderately busy roads

Difficulty F3 T3

Bike any bike

Access take E 45th Ave 1.5 km E from Victoria Dr, or 1.6 km W from Boundary Rd; or follow Rupert St/Kerr St to E 45th Ave and head W 1 block

Short Description a ride past the greenery of Champlain Heights, the oldest continuously operating dairy in BC, and a pretty urban lake park

ROAD LOG

0.0 Killarney St at E 45th Ave — Albert Massey Field, NW corner of Killarney Pk; head S

0.1 curve right on E 46th Ave

0.2 left on Raleigh St

0.5 right on E 48th Ave

0.7 left on Vivian St

1.6 left on E 57th Ave along Fraserview Golf Course

1.7 right on Rosemont Dr.

2.3 cross Kerr St

Option: for Everett Crowley Pk, head S on Kerr St just past E 63rd Ave to find entrance on left; or enter from E 62nd Ave where it curves into Butler St

2.8 right on Butler St

2.9 left on Maquinna Dr. (becomes Tyne St at E 54th Ave)

4.7 left on E 45th Ave

5.2 right on McKinnon St

5.6 cross E 41st Ave (patience)

5.7 curve left on School Ave, then right on McKinnon St to pass the four Carleton Schools

5.9 cross Kingsway (to NE at 3201: Carleton Cycle in rustic wooden building (438-6371))

6.2 left on Euclid Ave

Caution: *unsigned intersections ahead*

Carleton School #4.

7.1 right on Earles St

7.3 cross over Skytrain

7.5 Earles curves into Nootka St, then Boyd Div.

8.1 Renfrew Ravine Pk on left, Boyd Div. curves into Renfrew St, Renfrew Pk on right

8.6 left on E 18th Ave (across from tennis courts)

9.4 right on Copley St

9.7 left on E 15th Ave

9.8 cross Nanaimo St; **Caution: *poor alignment***

10.0 continue on gravel into John Hendry Pk, curve left on paved 7-Eleven Bicycle Trail; washrooms, concession, swimming

10.4	straight to cross parking lot and leave via access road
10.6	left on E 19th Ave
10.7	right on Gladstone St
10.9	left at Skytrain to go under it, then at Walker St do a sharp right onto Vanness Ave
11.1	left on Gladstone St
11.6	keep right at Brock St; cross Kingsway
11.9	angle left on Gladstone at junction of E 30th Ave and E 31st Ave
12.3	left on E 34th Ave
13.0	right on Slocan St
13.3	left on E 38th Ave
13.5	right on Wales St
13.8	cross E 41st Ave
14.0	5805 on right: Avalon Dairy, Mon-Fri 9 am-5:30 pm, Sat 9 am-5 pm; closed Hol (434-2434)
14.0	5872 on left: *Cooper House*
14.2	left on E 45th Ave
14.6	conclude trip at Albert Massey Field

The blossoms of the cherries and flowering plums add a dainty touch to the still-stark landscape of early spring as you cycle the streets of Killarney and Fraserview. Heading into Champlain Heights, the strips of woodland left during development are a welcome touch.

Avalon Dairy: nearly a century of family run business.

Just to the south of your route is a relatively new and little-known park honouring Everett Crowley, son of the founder of Avalon Dairy. Vancouver's fourth largest park, it perches atop a landfill site abandoned over a quarter century ago. Alder and blackberries are among the predominant vegetation.

Coming into Collingwood, you pass the four Carleton schools, all built within eight years. The smallest building, Vancouver's only remaining one-room schoolhouse, dates from 1905. Two years later the school's capacity was tripled with construction of what is now the oldest two-room school in the city. The other wooden building was built in 1908; its two identical siblings, separated at birth, are Selkirk School #1 (1750 E 22nd Ave) and Brock School #2 (4860 Main St). Carleton School #4 was built of brick, in 1911-12.

Continuing on the other side of Kingsway, the road is once again flanked with flowering plums. Having come downhill past bushy Renfrew Ravine Park and more-open Renfrew Park, you encounter yet more attractive street trees on your way to lovely John Hendry Park. The trail through the park itself passes large weeping willows and maples.

Remember when milk was delivered to the door in reusable glass bottles? Avalon Dairy still does so, and although they now use trucks, one of the old delivery wagons stands out front as a reminder of the time when they used horses instead of gas. Established in 1906, Avalon is the oldest continuously operating — and the oldest family-run — dairy in BC, a holdout from the neighbourhood's rural days. Preservative-free ice cream is sold here too, but only by the tub — shouldn't be a problem if you brought friends.

Hiding across the street behind massive chestnut trees stands the 1919 *Cooper House*. Preserving its original setback on 0.4 ha, this handsome Craftsman home complements Avalon's simpler aspect.

Things certainly have changed since the time when the only two east-west roads between Westminster Road (Kingsway) and River Road (Marine Drive) were No 1 Road (E 45th Ave) and No 2 Road (E 54th Ave), and hefty fir planks were used in place of asphalt!

In the days when Vancouver wasn't even a name on the map, the boilers of the steam engines at Hastings Mill on Burrard Inlet received their water via flume from Trout Lake. Although you wouldn't guess by looking at it today, the shores of Trout Lake were once densely wooded. In later years, most of the land that was to become John Hendry Park was donated to the city by Mrs E.W. Hamber, daughter of John Hendry, part-owner of the Hastings Mill. Long popular for summer swimming, it wasn't until the 1950s that the site was cleared of brush, giving way to the large grassy areas of the present.

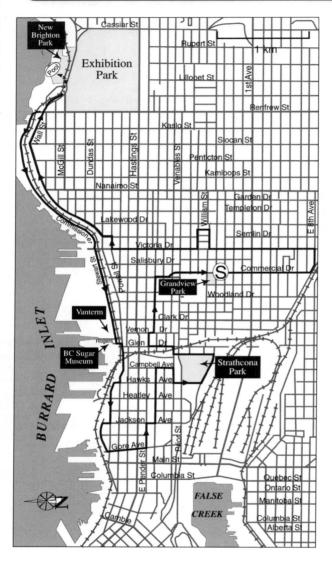

Distance and Elev Gain	17.6 km, 125 m, return
Terrain, Road, Traffic	gentle ups and downs; paved except for a short section, mostly on low-moderate traffic city streets with 2.4 km on busier roads
Difficulty	F2 T4
Bike	any bike
Access	Commercial Drive is 3.4 km W of Boundary Rd and 2.3 km E

of Main St while Charles St is 4 blocks N of 1st Ave. Prior St and 1st Ave are not great for cycling so if you're cycling from home, you may want to start the route at the point nearest to you. (Route V15)

Short Description a trip passing unique restaurants, boutiques, and heritage buildings of the colourful East Side and waterfront, with visits to the site of first white settlement in Vancouver, a cargo terminal, and a sugar museum.

ROAD LOG

0.0 Commercial Dr. at Charles St, SE corner of Grandview Pk; head S

1.1 left on Grandview Hwy N, along railway cut

1.2 left on E 8th Ave

1.4 left on Victoria Dr.

2.6 right on William St; 1972 is one of many fine old homes

2.8 left on Rose St; enjoy the community spirit!

2.9 left on Napier St, St Francis of Assisi on right

3.2 right on Victoria Dr.; turreted homes

3.9 cross E Hastings St, old brick pavement

4.2 right on Triumph St

4.4 left on Semlin Dr.

4.5 cross Dundas St, then right on Wall St

6.3 cross N Renfrew St

6.6 left through parking lot just before McGill St

6.9 left downhill, narrow tunnel

7.1 New Brighton Pk, pool (swimming free Mon-Fri 11:30 am-5:15 pm), plaque near W end of pool office; **return by same route**

7.5 right on Wall St

7.8 right on Commissioner St (later becomes Stewart St), overpass; **Caution: *several diagonal railway* crossings**

10.3 Caution: *brief narrowing*

10.6 Vanterm public viewing platform, displays, film; Tue-Fri 9 am-noon & 1-4 pm (666-6129)

11.0 left on Rogers St; for BC Sugar Museum detour 120 m right instead, then 50 m left through gate and under the overpass to brown awning on right; Mon-Fri 9 am-4 pm (253-1131), plant dates from 1904-24

11.1 right on Powell St

11.6 right on Hawks Ave, curve left on Alexander St; 1921-23 Ballantyne Pier warehouses visible to right — get a closer look via Heatley St overpass

12.1 right on Jackson Ave

12.2 left on Railway St

Rose St: home to cat lovers.

12.4   pass Dunlevy Ave; at 50 to right: Missions to Seamen, 1905 office of Hastings Mill

12.5   left on Gore Ave; interesting older buildings

12.8   cross E Cordova St; St James Church on left, Firehall Theatre on right (689-0926), Vancouver Police Centennial Museum/Coroner's Court on right at 240 E Cordova ($2, Mon-Fri (+ Sat in summer) 11:30 am-4:30 pm, 665-3346)

13.0   left on E Pender St

13.3   right on Jackson Ave; on left: 1897 brick-faced Lord Strathcona School #2, city's oldest remaining school

13.4   left on Keefer St

14.0   right on Campbell Ave

14.2   right on Union St

14.4   left on Hawks Ave, walk through small park, cross Prior St

14.6   Strathcona Community Gardens on right, Strathcona Pk on left

14.7   left on Malkin Ave, fruit and vegetable warehouses

15.1   left on Raymur Ave

Modern cranes flank '20's warehouses at Ballantyne Pier.

15.5   cross Venables St, then right on Union St

15.7   left on Glen Dr

15.8   on right: 1907 Seymour Public School #2

16.0   right on E Pender St, passing 1900 Seymour School #1, oldest wooden school in Vancouver

16.1   right on Vernon Dr., then left on Frances St, stone cobbles

16.3   cross Clark Dr (use care)

16.8   right on Commercial Dr., curve left

17.6   back at start

Mention Commercial Drive to an East-Sider, and you'll instantly invoke fond thoughts of favourite eateries and cappuccino bars, cherished night spots, unique little boutiques and markets, and festivals. It is a focus for both Italian and Latin-American culture in the city. As you survey its offerings on your way through, choose a place (or several) to come back to on your return.

Doubling back north on Victoria Drive, you find some fine homes of the early 1900s. Of the many corner groceries that seemingly sprang randomly from the ground in the misty time before zoning regulations, only a few are managing to survive modern preferences for the mega store over community shopping. A detour past more heritage homes takes you down Rose Street with its colourful signs.

On the way to New Brighton Park, Wall Street leads past pleasant little parks overlooking the activities in Burrard Inlet. From this historical park site, the route continues along the industrialized waterfront. For a window on the operations of a modern container terminal, visit the viewing platform and interpretation area at Vanterm. Also worth a visit is the Sugar Museum. Here you will find the fascinating history of sugar and its processing, and of B.T. Rogers, the man who brought it to Vancouver.

After passing the city's oldest remaining dock warehouses at Ballantyne Pier, and the 1905 office of Hastings Mill (now serving as Missions to Seamen), you head inland towards the east end of Chinatown's spirited commercial core. En route watch for interesting buildings such as massively built St James Anglican Church and the unusual Georgian Revival Coroner's Court.

Strathcona, one of Vancouver's first neighbourhoods, began as a study in contrasts, a rich mixture of big and small, wealthy and poor, residential and commercial. Over the years it became home to successive waves of immigrants from Britain, Italy, Scandinavia, Eastern Europe, and China. That so much of this colourful community survives is a credit to its tenacious residents; when City Hall tried to fulfil its 1958 20-year plan dictating that the entire area be razed and replaced with large, sterile housing projects and freeway schemes, they collectively stood up and said "NO!" Think of these spirited people and the pioneers who preceded them as you ride past their bright green, blue, yellow, red, and pink old homes, the venerable schools, and the Strathcona Community Gardens.

The Fraser River at New Westminster was never a good choice for swimming, even back in the 1860s. Thus, when the Douglas Road was completed in 1865, the wealthier denizens of the capital soon took to braving a bumpy 16 km stagecoach ride to spend their weekends swimming, dancing, and drinking at what would soon be one of BC's top two resorts (the other being Harrison Hot Springs). It was dubbed "New Brighton," after the English holiday beach, and Oliver Hocking's hotel became the Brighton Hotel. In 1869 the settlement was renamed Hastings, and the hotel likewise. Subsequently, entrepreneur George Black built the New Brighton Hotel.

Although its fame dwindled when it was bypassed by the CPR in 1887, Hastings townsite boasted many of Vancouver's "firsts," including the first white settler, cricket ground, customs, telephone, post office, pier, bridge, and museum. It also served as a departure point for loggers and mill workers who, on reaching the end of the road, would take the Sea Foam west to Stamp's Mill (later to be the Hastings Mill, at the foot of today's Dunlevy Street) or across the inlet to the thriving mill at Moodyville (1.5 km east of the foot of Lonsdale Avenue).

All but forgotten as a resort, New Brighton beach is now closed to swimmers, except in the park's outdoor pool.

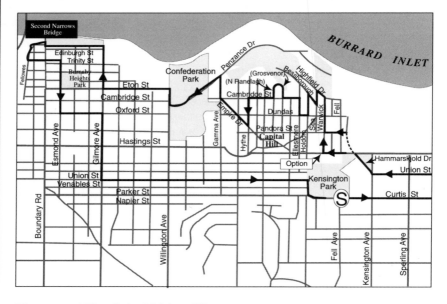

Distance and Elev Gain	25.0 km, 550 m, return
Terrain, Road, Traffic	up and down, steep in places; paved, but with 1.2 km on unpaved trails; mostly on quieter residential roads although 5.6 km can be moderately busy
Difficulty	F5 T4
Bike	you'd better have low gears and good brakes
Access	from Lougheed Hwy/Hwy 7, head about 0.1 km N on Holdom Ave, go 0.4 km E on Sumas St, and follow Fell Ave N to Curtis St
Short Description	a challenging route that climbs to the summits of North Burnaby, yielding panoramic views, with a visit to the Playground of the Gods

ROAD LOG

0.0	Curtis St at Kensington Pk Rink, just E of Fell Ave; head E
2.5	keep right on Curtis Extension
3.5	keep straight to cross Gaglardi Way; **Caution: *merging traffic***
4.8	Discovery Pk (high-tech industries) on left
6.3	keep right along N edge of campus
7.0	ride-sharing waiting shelters
7.2	bike path begins, but take instead the parallel gravel path on the right (OK, you can keep to the roads for extra climbing)

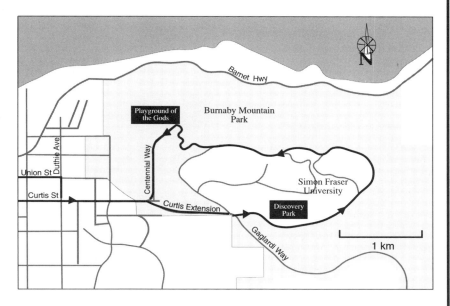

7.7   enter woods, passing barrier and boulders; keep straight past concrete reservoir on
       left, then angle right to follow fence into Burnaby Mountain Pk (walk if congested);
       viewpoints

8.4   left towards parking and Horizons Restaurant, passing Playground of the Gods

8.5   right to join parking lot; keep right to descend on Centennial Way

9.5   right on Curtis St (a wider road would be nice)

10.5   right on Duthie Ave

10.8   left on Union St

12.0   angle right on Hammarskjold Dr. at
       Kensington Ave

12.3   cross Hastings St to continue on gravel
       trail (patience)
       Option: left on Hastings St, right on
       Warwick Ave

12.7   left on Pandora St

12.9   right on Warwick Ave

13.3   left on Highfield Dr.

13.5   left on N Sea Rd

13.7   right on Bessborough Dr.

13.8   left on N Holdom Ave

14.1   right on Dundas St (especially steep!)

14.2   right on N Ellesmere Ave

14.4   left on Cambridge St

*Quiet roads add to Capitol Hill's
appeal for a scenic workout.*

14.6	right on N Grosvenor Ave, pass park, and return on N Ranelagh Ave
15.0	right on Cambridge St (fairly steep)
15.2	great viewpoint at Harbourview Rd
15.3	left on N Hythe Ave
15.7	sharp right on Empire Dr.
16.1	angle right on N Gamma Ave
16.4	left on Penzance Dr.
16.6	Confederation Pk
17.1	right on N Willingdon Ave
17.3	left on Eton St
18.1	right on N Gilmore Ave
18.6	curve left on lane beyond Edinburgh St
19.2	right on Boundary Rd, go around end, curve left on Fellowes St (traffic viewpoint)
19.7	left up Trinity Ave (especially steep!)
19.9	cross Boundary Rd, continue on lane
20.1	right on N Esmond St; 401 on right: *Over Lynn*, 1912, handsome stone and half-timbered
20.2	Burnaby Heights Pk on left; washrooms, fountain
20.5	pass barrier at Cambridge St
20.6	left on Oxford St; 3814 on right: a stately heritage home from 1912
21.1	right on N Gilmore Ave
21.2	50 on left: decorative Gilmore Secondary School
21.5	cross Hastings (busier)
22.0	left on Union St
24.4	right on Holdom Ave
24.6	left on Curtis St
25.0	back in front of Kensington Rink
	More information: Burnaby Parks and Recreation: 294-7450

North Burnaby: great views of the North Shore mountains.

Be prepared for a bit of a workout on this route, with most of the steepest parts being on Capitol Hill. The climb up to Simon Fraser University takes you the highest, however, and you'll probably wish that the paved shoulder began a little lower and continued all the way up, but it's not too bad outside of peak hours.

Burnaby Mountain was logged years ago; the regrowth has been mostly alder woods and petroleum tank farms, but residential areas have been steadily expanding. The mountain's trails have been discovered by hikers and mountain bikers; some students even use them for commuting. The steep north side can be treacherous, however.

Simon Fraser University, on the summit, broke with tradition in many ways when it opened in 1965. Although its architecture appears unconventional, architects Arthur Erickson and Geoffrey Massey are said to have drawn from traditional sources such as Greek palaestras, Buddhist temples, and Christian monasteries in its design.

The views are somewhat limited by the young alders, but this privation is soon rectified after a shortcut to Burnaby Mountain Park. From this 280-metre high vantage point you can contemplate Belcarra, Mount Seymour, and far peaks, or look down to the tiny ships plying Burrard Inlet at your feet. Just to the west stand the sculptures of Nuburi Toko.

Descending from Burnaby Mountain, you meet your next challenge climbing Capitol Hill, named to suggest an air of gentility. Although it is only 200 metres high, the going is quite steep in places. Views back towards the east and northeast are the initial compensation. At the top is a small park where you just might want to collapse in the grass awhile if you're out of shape. Heading down the west side, you can look across the valley of Still Creek towards Metrotown, but the highlight is the unusual perspective towards downtown Vancouver, overlooking the rolling residential foreground. During the boom years of 1909-13, these views helped promoters sell the area as one of the most prestigious places to live in Greater Vancouver.

Continuing towards Vancouver past more tank farms, you'll find blackberries in season along the steep, bushy slopes leading down to Burrard Inlet. After one final lookout, above the teeming traffic making its way to and from the Second Narrows Bridge, it's time to head back. One more steep ascent brings you up to the first of two heritage buildings, and then it's fairly easy going the rest of the way, except for one last little hump.

High above Burrard Inlet stand over a dozen stark, carved poles and groupings both vaguely familiar yet stirringly exotic. They are the totems of the Ainu, the aboriginal people of Japan. To the carver, Nuburi Toko, Kamui Mintara (Playground of the Gods) *is "a poem of love," sharing with us his people's interpretation of the relationship between humanity and the gods. Like the First Peoples of North America, the Ainu have a mythology rich in creatures of divine origin. This exhibition commemorates the first quarter-century of friendship between the District of Burnaby and her sister city of Kushiro, Japan.*

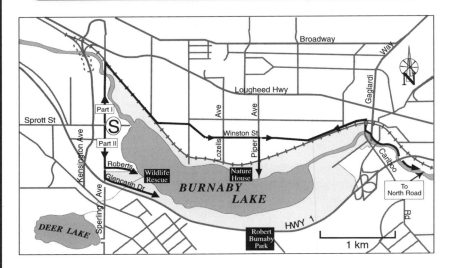

Distance and Elev Gain (Pt I) 15.6 km and (Pt II) 4.4 km, nil, return

Terrain, Road, Traffic some small ups and downs; paved, with 1 km on disused road, and 3.9 km on gravel; mostly on quieter roads but with 8.5 km on moderately-used roads

Difficulty F2 T3 and F1 T1

Bike any bike that will handle good gravel tracks

Access go E on Sprott St to Sperling Ave; Sprott St runs from Royal Oak Ave to just past Kensington Ave (Hwy 1 Exit 33 N) (best cycling access to Sprott St might be via Norland Ave) (Route V12)

Short Description exploring the shores of Burnaby Lake and Brunette River, with a visit to a "habitat garden"; lots of ducks and other birds, too

ROAD LOG

Part I

0.0 Sperling Ave at Sprott St, near Burnaby Lake Sports Complex; head N

0.4 straight on disused section of road "at your own risk"

0.7 cross bridge; **Caution: *holes in pavement***

0.8 gravel trail on left from Kensington overpass

0.9 right on Winston St; **Caution: *traffic from left***

1.0 large Dairyland plant on left

1.6 **Caution: *diag. railway crossing***

2.9 pass Lozells Ave; Dairyland Ice Cream Div. on right

3.4 right on Piper Ave

3.6 Warner Loat Pk on left, washrooms

3.9 Burnaby Lake Nature House on right, summer only (420-3031); beyond, at beginning of no-cycling zone, find self-serve grain sales; return same way

4.4 right on Winston St

6.0 right on Cariboo Rd

6.1 left on Cariboo Place (just before bridge)

6.4 pass green gate at end of cul-de-sac to continue on gravel trail

6.7 cross Stoney Creek on small bridge, to continue on gravel track

6.9 pass well beneath freeway

8.3 gate; beyond lurks noisy North Rd; return via same route (bypassing Piper Ave); use caution turning left off Cariboo Rd and left off Winston St to cross tracks at Sperling Ave

15.6 back at sports complex

Part II

0.0 Sperling Ave at Sprott St, near Burnaby Lake Sports Complex; head S

0.5 left on Roberts St

1.0 Rowing Pavilion and bleachers

1.5 left on Sperling Ave

1.9 curve left on Glencarin Dr.

2.5 5216 on left: Wildlife Rescue Association, Sept-Mar: 9 am-5 pm, Apr-Aug: 8 am-7:30 pm (526-7275)

2.7 end of road, pedestrians and equestrians only on sawdust trail; **return via same route** (bypassing Roberts St)

Waterfowl thrive along Burnaby Lake's marshy shore.

4.4 finished

More information: Burnaby Parks and Recreation (from Rowing Pavilion N but S of Still Ck): 294-7450, GVRD Parks (the rest of the lake and shores): 520-6442

The rich brown tint of the water that gives the Brunette River its name is caused not by modern industrial effluents but by seepage from the ancient peat beds that lie beneath Burnaby Lake, from whence the river flows. Regardless of the water's colour, fish — steelhead, cutthroat, coho, sculpin, chubb, and others — were all plentiful in the river, the lake, and its tributaries.

As industrialization materialized in the watershed, the Brunette became the Lower Mainland's most polluted river during the 1970s, and fish became scarce. Conditions have been slowly improving, with help from the students at Stoney Creek Community School and their yearly "Great Salmon Sendoff" festival (first fry released 1984), the Sapperton Fish and Game Club, and the BC Ministry of the Environment. However, only when everyone stops dumping

unwanted fluids down storm drains, and industrial discharge and spills are elimi-
nated, will the natural system fully recover.

Heading north, you take a disused section of road that is being reclaimed along
the edges by plants and shrubs. Watch for holes in the bridge across Still Creek!

Note: alternative route: take Kensington Ave bike route north to cross Still
Creek, then take the gravel trail east to the disused road; or stay on the bike
route to its confusing end and then cross Kensington to continue around the
loop and back south across Lougheed Hwy to Winston St, then turn left

A little further there is an unofficial, look-both-ways-and-carry-your-bike
railway crossing. Ice cream fans will be momentarily excited to discover
Dairyland's ice cream plant but sorry, no tours.

Some distance further, Warner Loat Park makes a good spot for picnicking
under the trees. During the summer, stop in to see what's happening at the
GVRD Nature House. At the lake shore itself you'll find many ducks right
along the path and in nearby Eagle Creek. For a wider perspective, climb the
observation tower, or wander out along the pier that reaches well past the marshy
edge and the water lilies. As well as many species of ducks, bird watchers have
seen bushtit, Bewick's wren, bald eagle, osprey, black-headed grosbeak, war-
blers, Virginia rail, western screech owl, and other birds in this area.

Continuing along, you come to a pleasant gravel track that follows the
Brunette Riverthrough wooded surroundings, with many places to eat
salmonberries (in the spring) or to sit and contemplate the water. At its end,
North Road (built as one of Colonel Moody's strategic 1859 access roads to
deep water) doesn't make for great cycling, so it's time to turn around.

Going south from the starting point takes you to the Rowing Pavilion, a fine
spot for views across the lake, or to watch budding rowing greats at practice.
Further along this side of the lake is the Wildlife Rescue Association. As with
any hospital, they don't put the patients on display, but do drop in at the gift
shop, and wander around the Habitat Garden to learn how you can make your
own garden more attractive to wildlife. The association always has opportunities for volunteers to help out.

The road goes only a little further, and then it's a choice of turning back or
continuing on foot.

---

*Although the District of Burnaby draws its name (through Burnaby Lake)
from Robert Burnaby, private secretary to Colonel Richard Moody of the
Royal Engineers for six months in 1858, he lived here only a short time
before moving to Victoria.*

RIGHT: At the Rowing Pavilion, Burnaby Lake.

V12 • Deer Lake

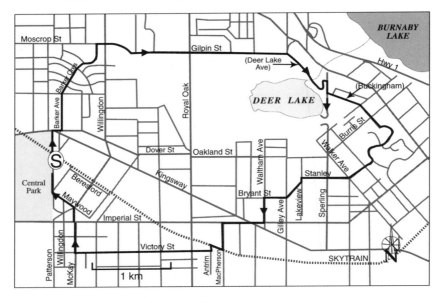

Distance and Elev Gain 13.6 km, 125 m, return

Terrain, Road, Traffic flat but with one each rather steep downhill and uphill; paved roads; mostly quiet-to-very-quiet but with 2.7 km on busier Moscrop/Gilpin St and Imperial St

Difficulty F2 T5

Bike gears recommended

Access from Willingdon Ave turn NW on Beresford St just S of Skytrain; bike only: follow the 7-Eleven Bicycle Route to Patterson Skytrain station (Route V13)

Short Description great but fleeting views, followed by visits to an urban lake park, an art gallery, an almost big-as-life model railway, and a fun, early-1900s main street reconstruction

ROAD LOG

0.0 E side of Central Pk, Patterson Ave at 7-Eleven Bicycle Trail; head N

0.3 cross Kingsway, curve right on Grange St (at NE corner of Central Pk is an old stone entrance arch from the (demolished) 1891 Vancouver Club Building)

0.5 left on Barker Ave

0.9 cross Burke St, angling right on Barker Cres, moderately steep descent with great but fleeting vista towards Coquitlam

1.8 right on Moscrop St (busier)

3.0 cross Royal Oak St; Moscrop becomes Gilpin St; **Caution: *narrow***

4.0 right on Deer Lake Ave as Deer Lake Place curves left to pass Municipal Hall

4.3 6344 on right: Burnaby Art Gallery, Tue-Fri: 9 am-5 pm, Sat-Sun/Hol 12-5 pm (291-9441)

4.5 6450 on right: James Cowan Theatre (291-6864)

4.7 4900 on left: Burnaby Central Railway, $1, 12-4:30 pm weekends Easter to Thanksgiving, daily Jul-Aug except Mon (291-0922)

4.8 6450 on right: Burnaby Arts Centre (291-6864) (also Mayfair House Potters' Guild Workshop)

4.9 lake shore access

5.0 6664 on right: Hart House restaurant (*Avalon*, built in 1912 as a country estate for F.J. Hart, real estate agent) (298-4278)

5.1 6501 on left: Deer Lake Heritage Pk/Burnaby Village Museum, $4.50, Apr-Sep and special occasions, 10 am to 5 pm (293-6501)

5.2 right on Sperling Ave; carefully use sidewalk to bypass cyclist-unfriendly intersection

5.5 entrance to Deer Lake Pk waterfront picnic area; boat rentals $6-$15/hr afternoons; no swimming

5.6 end of parking lot; left on Sperling Ave

5.8 right on Buckingham Ave; a ritzy part of Burnaby

6.5 cross Burris St; steepish slope

7.4 right on Stanley Ave

7.8 angle right at Walker St

8.4 left on Lakeview Ave, then angle right on Bryant St

8.7 cross Gilley Ave; watch for traffic from left

9.1 left on Waltham Ave

9.4 right on Imperial St (busier)

9.6 cross Kingsway/1A/99A

9.9 left on MacPherson Ave

10.2 right on Beresford St, just past Skytrain

10.4 left on Antrim Ave, then right on quiet Victory St

11.9 jog at Sussex Ave

12.2 right on McKay Ave

A relic steam donkey at Deer Lake Heritage Park

12.6 jog at Imperial St

12.8 left on Maywood St

12.9 cross Willingdon Ave (patience)

13.1 bypass barrier, then right on Patterson Ave; a few old houses remain in the emerging forest of skyscrapers

13.6 back at Skytrain

Is Deer Lake connected to False Creek by a water-filled tunnel? Pauline Johnson tells a curious tale in *Legends of Vancouver*. One day in the early 1800s, before the days of white settlement, the first Chief Capilano was out hunting in his canoe. In False Creek he spotted a seal, which with impeccable skill and practised arm he solidly speared. The seal dove and never resurfaced. The strong, woven rope and the attached spear vanished as well. Perplexed, the chief spent many hours searching for the seal and his cherished elk-bone spear, which had been handed down to him through three generations of hunters, but to no avail.

Colourful gardens complement the stately Burnaby Art Gallery.

About a year later, Chief Capilano was out in his canoe when he saw a strange glow in the sky. Tracing it to its source, he found a forest fire at Deer Lake. Looking around, he discovered dead on the shore the long-lost king of the seals, the precious spear still embedded in his flesh.

A century after Chief Capilano's miraculous experience, Henry and Grace Ceperley took a liking to the shores of Deer Lake. Their home, *Fairacres*, a majestic three-storey 1911-12 Tudor structure incorporating local cobblestones, became the house of its day in Burnaby. Today it houses the Burnaby Art Gallery, showing both prints from the permanent collection and temporary exhibits. Visit in spring and you'll find the rhododendrons in the back garden a blaze of red. Adjacent are the Burnaby Arts Centre, Mayfair House Potters' Guild Workshop and the James Cowan Theatre.

If you've always had a fascination for model railways, you'll love Burnaby Central Railway just down the road with its extensive outdoor layout. Just around the corner you'll find exquisite dining in the picturesque Tudor Hart House inn. Across the street is a treat for the history buff: Deer Lake Heritage Park. Here, days long past are brought back to life on a recreated turn-of-the-century street scene featuring a drug store, print shop, smithy, etc.

Deer Lake itself is pretty — a good place to watch the ducks or rent a boat, but too contaminated for swimming. The District of Burnaby is studying the problem of how to clean it up before it becomes a bog.

When Burnaby's Urban Trails plan is fully implemented, it will be much more relaxing to go to Deer Lake by bicycle. For now, part of the route in is often fairly busy. The way back to Central Park begins with a rather steep climb, but then continues largely on incredibly quiet residential roads.

RIGHT: Cooperation allows cyclists to share Central Park with other users. (Unlocked?! The owner must be nearby)

10 km/h MAXIMUM

BICYCLE ETIQUETTE

Pedestrians have the Right of Way and
Cyclists shall give way to Pedestrians at
all times.
Cyclists shall use the trails in single file only.
There shall be no racing of bikes.
Dismount areas shall be honoured by Cyclists.
A maximum speed limit of 6 m.p.h. (10 km.)
shall be observed by cyclists at all times.

Burnaby Parks & Recreation Commission

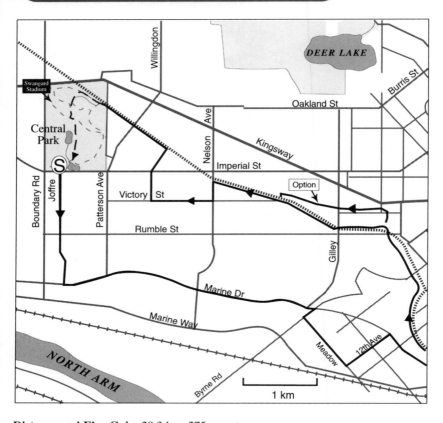

Distance and Elev Gain	29.3 km, 275 m, return
Terrain, Road, Traffic	rolling hills with one steep (short) climb and several steepish descents; mostly paved, with about 2 km on good gravel; largely on low-traffic secondary roads, but with about 4.9 km on busier Marine Dr. and about 8 km on trails/paths
Difficulty	F4 T4
Bike	any bike that can handle a bit of gravel and some climbing
Access	take Imperial St (continuation of Vancouver's E 49th Ave) to the point 0.2 km E of Boundary Rd in S Burnaby; or, by bike only, puzzle your way along the 7-Eleven Trail E from Vancouver to Central Pk (Route V12)
Short Description	a fairly rural approach to the heritage buildings and waterfront attractions of the Royal City, returning along the route of a tramline built over a century ago

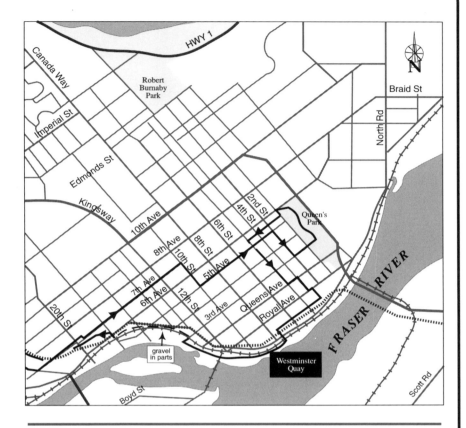

ROAD LOG

0.0 Joffre Ave at Imperial St, across from parking area at Central Pk; head S

0.1 keep straight at jog in road

0.2 pass Ocean View Cemetery and descend fairly steeply

1.6 left on Marine Dr.; **Caution: *some faster traffic, occasional black curb ridges***

2.3 4250 on right: New Haven Borstal (correctional) Institute

4.3 5462 on right: Hare Krishna Temple and Govinda's Natural Foods Restaurant, Mon-Sat noon-2 pm and 5 pm-8 pm (431-0165)

5.0 right on Byrne Rd

5.1 left on Meadow Ave

5.5 Burnaby and Region Allotment Garden on left

6.0 left on 12th Ave

6.7 right on Marine Dr. (short, steep climb!)

7.5 Schara-Tzedeck (Jewish) Cemetery on left

7.6 left on Trapp/7th Ave to pass 22nd St Station

8.2	walk across 20th St, resuming opposite in lane
8.3	right on Bowler St, then left on 7th Ave
8.4	Grimston Pk on right
9.6	cross 12th St **(use care)**
9.9	right on 10th St; Moody Pk on left, washrooms
10.1	cross 6th Ave **(use care)**
10.3	left on 5th Ave
10.6	cross 8th St **(use care)** to enter commercial heart of upper New Westminster
11.0	cross 5th St; (diversion — use crosswalk)
	Of the many older buildings, only a few of the highlights have been selected.
11.3	237 5th Ave on left: 1894, exemplary Victorian Queen Anne Revival
11.5	right on 2nd St (divided)
11.8	325 2nd St on left: 1910-11, basically Prairie Style
11.9	314 2nd St on right: 1908, Classical Revival; left on 3rd Ave
12.1	238 1st St on right, 1904, *Bunachie*, Classical Revival, built for Mrs George McKay, a then-recently-widowed single parent, using proceeds from a laundry she ran next door; she rented it out for eight years and then moved in
12.1	cross 1st St to enter Queen's Pk
12.3	turn left past stadium and arena, just before Arenex
12.6	through archway into Centennial Grove (1860-1960); keep straight to bypass parking
13.0	sharp left on 1st St; **Caution: *traffic turning off 6th Ave***
13.1	right on Regina St
13.6	left on 4th St
13.8	431 4th St on left: 1890, elegant Queen Anne Revival
14.0	403 4th Ave, on right: 1901, *Melbourne*, outstanding Queen Anne Revival
14.0	335 4th St on left: 1892, elegant *Homestead*
14.2	317 3rd Ave on left: Carlton Court, 1925 apartment block
14.4	left on Queens Ave; Tipperary Pk on right
14.6	right on 3rd St; first on large-aggregate concrete slabs, then on cobbles; 125 3rd St on left: 1905, simplified Queen Anne Revival, built for "Mr May Day," J.J. Johnston, who attended every May Day celebration from his birth in 1870 'til his death in 1966
14.7	left on Royal Ave (use crosswalk)
14.8	302 Royal Ave on right: Irving House and New Westminster Museum, donation, May-Sep: Tue-Sun 11 am-5 pm (rest of year: weekends 1 pm-5 pm) (521-7656)
14.8	right on Merivale St
15.0	right on Carnarvon St
15.2	321 Carnarvon St on right: Emmanuel Pentecostal Church, 1889, restored red brick, formerly St Andrew's Presbyterian; adjacent is 1863 wooden church, the first Presbyterian one on BC mainland
15.4	514 on left: Holy Trinity Cathedral, 1899, fortress-like tower, based on St Paul's, Kensington, UK
15.6	630-2 on left: (Environment Canada Sediment Survey), 1906; 653 across the street: new court house and Begbie Square, with a statue of His Lordship The

Honourable Sir Matthew Baillie Begbie; 668 on left is Begbie Court, comprising the impressive old provincial court house, 1899, and land registry offices, 1910

15.7   left on Begbie St; 740 Carnarvon on right: College Place Hotel, 1907 (originally the Russell Hotel), Classical Revival, was soon acknowledged as the city's premier hotel; fairly steep descent

16.0   right along waterfront, past tugs, sight-seeing boats, the MV *Expo Tugger* for children

16.1   pass Westminster Quay, a marketplace offering fresh produce, handicrafts, baked goodies, restaurant fare for almost any taste

16.3   *Samson V*, a former snag-puller and last of the steam paddlewheelers, weekends & Hol 12-5 pm (summer: Wed-Sun) (522-6894 or 521-7656)

16.4   continue along waterfront on 7-Eleven Bicycle Trail, somewhat bumpy
Cautions for entire 7-Eleven Trail: *pedestrians may be encountered, not all curbs are dropped, use care at road crossings*

17.1   Quayside Pk, drinking fountain; beyond is 1911 railway bridge to Queensborough; curve right and turn left on Quayside Dr. (curb)

17.4   **Caution: *angled tracks***

17.7   curve right on moderately steep overpass

17.9   left on 7-Eleven Trail (through parking lots) just before Stewardson Way

18.2   cross 14th St and continue on gravel

18.7   water fountain

18.8   jog at tracks

19.1   tedious two step crossing of Stewardson Way

19.4   officially, the 7-Eleven Trail goes uphill and left on 7th Ave to 22nd St; many cyclists cross 20th St immediately, take the narrow gravel trail to 22nd St Station and carefully follow outside of bus loop to 22nd St and 7th Ave

One of the many fine heritage homes in New West.

19.8   right (W) from 22nd St and 7th Ave on gravel trail, soon paved

20.4   poor alignment at London St

20.5   great views to S and W (note red-black-white chimney of controversial GVRD garbage incinerator along Fraser at Big Bend); crickets in late summer

20.7   Skytrain repair and test facility on right

21.8   to left at 20th St and 20th Ave is Cliff's Honey Farm (521-3478)

22.1   left on other side of Rumble St at Skytrain
Option: take upper path, which turns N to cross Prenter and Beresford, then heads W past fine 1914 Craftsman style Kingsway East School located at Burnaby South Secondary and crosses Buller Ave 1.4 km later to rejoin the main route; (curbs not dropped)

22.9   cross Gilley Ave at Rumble St crosswalk, angle right

23.1	left on Irmin St, then right on Prenter St; **Caution: *diag. railway tracks***
23.5	cross Buller Ave
23.9	cross MacPherson Ave (might as well stay on road); **Caution: *diag. railway tracks***
24.7	left on Nelson Ave (to bypass poor section of 7-Eleven Trail)
25.1	right on Victory St
25.9	right on Sussex Ave
26.2	cross Imperial St (use care)
26.6	left on Beresford St, rejoining 7-Eleven Trail at disused bus access
27.1	cross Willingdon St (bothersome detour right to pushbutton light and back); continue on road
27.6	cross Patterson Ave into Central Pk (Route V12)
28.0	bear left on gravel at X (then keep to wide main trail through park)
28.2	bend left to merge with another trail
28.5	straight at major junction to pass E of duck pond
28.9	right to cross bridge at N end of pond, then W to N end of parking lot
29.0	head S on access road
29.3	Imperial St; end of trip

It began in 1863 as a narrow trail barely wide enough for a horse and rider, hacked through the thick, ancient forest to bypass the frozen Fraser from New Westminster to the sea. Today the old North Arm Trail has become Marine Drive and though the tall trees have long since fallen to the loggers, there is greenery in the form of healthy second growth, primarily alder. Although it isn't overly wide, Marine Drive is an attractive cycling route to New Westminster, especially now that much of the through traffic detours via Marine Way.

Helping the area retain an agricultural character are the farmlands of the New Haven Borstal Institute, and the nearly 30 market gardens of Big Bend. From their 80 ha, these intensive growers provide much of Vancouver's beets, carrots, Chinese greens and other bunch vegetables, to the tune of two million dollars per year. (See also the area near Byrne Rd at Mandeville Ave.) For the greatest variety, however, you can't beat the Burnaby and Region Allotment Gardens. All of the 370 plots (1991) have been allocated to people who otherwise wouldn't have space to grow their own vegetables.

Spiritual colour is added by the Hare Krishna Temple, with its flamboyant, giant-size statue of Lord Chaitanya, and also by an immaculate Jewish cemetery dating from 1929.

A little west of the centre of New Westminster is Moody Park, named after Colonel Richard Moody, commanding officer of the Royal Engineers, who laid out the streets of the city. Further east is beautiful Queens Park. Although much changed over the past 130 years, it remains the "People's Park" envisioned by Moody in 1860.

New Westminster had by 1912 become famous for its beautiful Victorian and Edwardian homes. Contributing to this fame were the adjoining gardens and tree-lined streets. Many of these early homes remain, especially in the vicinity of Queens Park, and have been complemented by fine examples from following decades. The oldest house still standing, splendidly preserved, is the 1862 Irving House. Built of California redwood for the era's quintessential riverboat master, Captain William Irving, this rare example of Gothic Revival architecture is furnished in the styles current from 1864-1890, including even some original wallpaper. Unobtrusively to the rear stands an extensive museum in which to further your exploration of the past.

Lower on the slope is the commercial district, almost all of which dates from after the great fire of 1898. Across from today's courthouse, Sir Matthew Baillie Begbie once maintained law and order as BC's first judge. The waterfront, previously the site of salmon canneries and sawmills, is quickly being swallowed up by condos and apartments, but also features a large market and a promenade.

The return trip along the 7-Eleven Bicycle Trail follows fairly closely the route of the 1891 Central Park Tramline that linked Vancouver and New Westminster until 1953. A good idea in principle, the 7-Eleven Trail falls a little short of many cyclists' ideals; the most appealing section is between 22nd St Station and Rumble St.

The gold fever of 1858 saw American prospectors swarming up the Fraser River in search of the mother lode. James Douglas, Chief Factor of the Hudson's Bay Co. Western Division and a staunch British patriot, grew worried and sent to Britain for assistance. In November of 1858 a ceremony at Fort Langley commemorated the appointment of Douglas as Governor of the new colony of British Columbia.

Colonel Richard Moody, commander of the Royal Engineers, considered Douglas's choice of Derby (near Fort Langley) as capital of the new colony to be too vulnerable to flooding and American attack. Moody chose instead a site further downstream, on high ground on the north side of the Fraser. To resolve a dispute over the naming of the new capital, Queen Victoria was consulted. She christened it "New Westminster," after her favourite part of London; by this kindness also giving it the epithet "The Royal City." Although the government of the newly amalgamated colonies of Vancouver Island and British Columbia decided in 1867 that Victoria would be the joint capital, residents of New Westminster can still proudly call their home the Royal City.

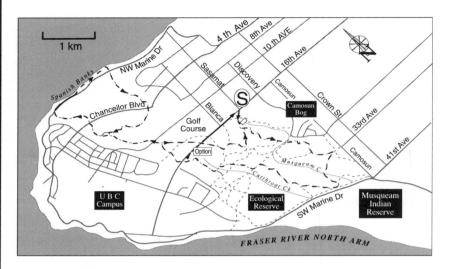

Distance and Elev Gain	16.6 km, 175 m, return
Terrain, Road, Traffic	generally up or down, with one steep climb; about 0.6 km on the road while the rest is hard-packed dirt trails with occasional gravel, rooty, rutty, muddy, or cobbly sections; heavily used by cyclists, walkers, joggers, and occasional equestrians
Difficulty	F4 T1
Bike	mountain bike recommended, esp. for N part
Access	head W on W 16th Ave towards UBC, or E from SW Marine Dr. on W 16th Ave (Routes V5, V6)
Short Description	a forest ride through the largest urban park in North America (and perhaps the world), with a visit to a sandy swimming beach; salal, red huckleberries, and salmonberries in season

ROAD LOG

Note: Major trails through PSRP are mostly well signposted with their names and use. Please respect any changed designations and use alternative trails as required.

0.0 W 16th Ave across from S end of Sasamat St at map board; head S, angling right on Sasamat Trail

0.2 skirt reservoir corner

0.4 take left fork at Huckleberry

1.3 bear left across Imperial (Route V5)

1.8 more challenging zig-zags

2.0 keep left at Hemlock

2.3 sharply right on Clinton at entrance to Clinton Stables clearing

2.8 cross Musqueam (formerly Tin Can) Creek

3.1 right on Salish, keep right (Route V6)

3.9 ecological reserve on left

4.8 left along power line cut (Imperial)

5.0 right on Salish

5.4 cross Council

5.6 bear left to cross Cutthroat Ck

5.7 curve right on main trail

6.2 curve left on main trail

6.3 keep right on Salish

6.5 jog left parallel to W 16th Ave, then cross, jog left again, then right to cross ditch and paved bike path

   Option: back to start — turn right on Sherry Sakamoto Trail

6.7 keep right at fork

7.1 keep right at fork

7.2 cross gravel parking lot and University Blvd, angle left just W of golf course

8.2 pass Spanish

8.6 cross paved bike path and Chancellor Blvd, take school driveway to cul-de-sac, angle left past barrier

9.1 trail becomes rutted and steeper

9.4 right on NW Marine Dr.

10.0 angle left on Seaside Route along Spanish Banks beach

10.2 Bicentennial Memorial

10.9 cross parking lot at midpoint (and NW Marine Dr.) to take Spanish Trail

11.1 trail climbs quite steeply: good test of climbing ability, but watch for people coming down!

11.9 keep left at fork

12.1 right angle onto bridge, then cross Chancellor Blvd (detour W) and continue opposite

12.9 first of 3 bumpy bridges (and one normal)

13.3 left on Salish

13.6 bear left at fork

13.9 cross University Blvd, left along parking lot onto Cleveland Trail

14.5 cross Heron Trail

14.7 pass park Visitor Centre

14.8 cross 16th Ave, bear slightly left into woods; **Caution: *tortuous/dim***

The wooded trails of Pacific Spirit Regional Park draw cyclists from all over.

Ride the trails of Pacific Spirit Regional Park for relaxation, and to enjoy the beauty and variety of the forest. With the exception of the part north of Chancellor Boulevard, this is a fairly easy ride. It begins by the reservoir, highest spot in the park, amongst sturdy second-growth conifers. Mostly gentle and smooth but at times steeper and rockier, the trail descends through colourful deciduous woods that include locally rare trembling aspen and conveniently placed huckleberry and salmonberry bushes.

A charming new life for a retired bike.

Beyond the disappearing grassy area where Clinton Stables once stood, the conifers once again become dense. The many decaying stumps, often fire-blackened, indicate that the area was once logged. Here and there a torpid creek lazily carries water towards the Fraser River. Just above Marine Drive is another former opening rapidly being overgrown by a thicket of vigorous young alders.

Back among the evergreens, it's gently uphill past the ecological reserve. These trees are second-growth, since 1890s logging. Just the other side of Imperial, the tall, straight Douglas firs grow so densely that you see little besides tree trunks. A little further, and the slowly rotting, reddish-brown stumps of ancient red cedars are everywhere, many with umbrellas of red huckleberry. You enter a moist deciduous stand, mostly alder and maple, where everything is festooned with moss. Suddenly, back among the conifers, there's a stretch where undergrowth is almost completely absent.

If time or enthusiasm is running out, the Sherry Sakamoto Trail is a convenient route back to your start.

On the north side of West 16th Avenue, the woods grow less dense. Beyond University Boulevard, smaller alders and underbrush predominate: a legacy to an aborted 1950s subdivision. The trail becomes narrower and rootier. Wider at first, the trail down towards Spanish Banks follows a steep-sided ravine through woods of greater stature and variety, becoming steeper and rutted towards the bottom.

A relaxing rest on the sandy beach at Spanish Banks gives you a chance to prepare for the steep climb just ahead, parts of which may actually be unrideable. The trail soon levels out a little, though. Conifers and salal become more plentiful and it gets muddy in places. As you bump along, watch out for the especially bumpy bridges south of Chancellor Boulevard.

Stop in at the Visitor Centre to find out more about the park and future plans, then continue, at first on a dim and slightly tortuous section, to ride the last couple kilometres of the route.

People had been using the wooded trails west of the city limits for years, but during the late 1980s concern over ongoing encroachment came to a head. When the dust settled in late 1988, 763 ha of the University Endowment Lands had been vested in the Greater Vancouver Regional District Parks Department as a regional park.

As Pacific Spirit Regional Park, the area became even more popular. Although this park is nearly twice the size of Stanley Park, the GVRD immediately found itself challenged in meeting the demands of the various users; hikers, joggers, naturalists, equestrians, orienteers, forestry students, nudists, mountain bikers, and other groups all had claims on the park's limited resources.

With public consultation, the GVRD produced a management plan. The first two years, 1992 and 1993, will be especially crucial for mountain bikers; during this period the future of cycling within the park will be assessed, based on the success of education and enforcement programs (including fines up to $100 that can escalate to $2000 if you don't pay) aimed at ensuring compatibility with other park values. Continued bicycle access to the park depends on everyone's using designated trails only and respecting other trail users.

Distance and Elev Gain	35.2 km, 225 m, return
Terrain, Road, Traffic	fairly flat with one steepish slope, several mild inclines and descents; mostly paved roads, occasionally rough, but with 3.7 km on bicycle path (some pavers and 0.5 km of gravel); mostly low traffic with about 6.7 km on moderate-heavy traffic roads (largely on Commercial/Victoria Dr.)
Difficulty	F3 T5
Bike	any bike
Access	from downtown, take Burrard Bridge, then right to foot of Chestnut St; from W 4th Ave or Cornwall Ave, take Cypress St N to Ogden Ave and turn right; bike only: join anywhere along city's Seaside Route on S side of False Ck (Routes V2, V3, V5, V6, V7, V9)
Short Description	a ride past some of Vancouver's tastiest bakeries and other purveyors of dessert items

ROAD LOG

Attention! *Experts advise you to feel comfortable leaving this longish route if you feel your taste buds tiring.*

0.0	foot of Chestnut St at Seaside Route; head diag. NE on good gravel
0.5	two boat launch crossings, then deke right on paved road, and immediately left on bike lane
0.9	under Burrard Bridge
1.0	left on road at cul-de-sac
1.3	keep straight where road curves right, then turn left; curve right to follow shore
1.6	cross Anderson St under Granville St Bridge — nip over to Granville Island (left) if you can't hold out until the first bakery right on the route — keep straight along shore (Route V2)
2.2	silly bicycle U-turn (wrong way down one-way street!)
2.5	left some 50 m to rejoin waterfront
3.4	left at cul-de-sac just beyond Monk McQueen's to rejoin waterfront
3.7	right on Spyglass Pl. just before Cambie Bridge
4.1	left on Commodore Rd (becomes 1st Ave)
4.6	right on Columbia St
5.3	left on 8th Ave
5.9	Main St; 2419 to right: Kam's Bakery (and restaurant) lots of delicious cream pastries, Chinese-type cookies, and buns; Mon-Sat 7 am-7 pm, Sun 7 am-6 pm; go left (N) to cross Main St on crosswalk; 2402 Main St: Bains Chocolates, a well-stocked old-fashioned style candy and chocolate store at this location since the mid '40s; Mon-Sat 10 am-5 pm; then take another crosswalk across Kingsway
6.0	left along Kingsway, then right on E 7th Ave
6.3	right on Brunswick St; small park on left, with benches
6.4	roundabout, left on E 8th Ave
7.2	left on St Catherines St
7.3	right on E 7th, passing China Creek Park
7.7	pass Vancouver Community College, former site of China Creek Bicycle Track; climb fairly steeply
7.9	cross Clark Dr. with care; **Caution: *unsigned intersections ahead***
8.2	left on Woodland Dr.
8.8	pedestrian light at E 1st Ave, **Caution: *rougher roads and unsigned intersections ahead***
9.3	left on William St
9.3	right on McLean Dr. (rough road)
9.6	cross Venables St (slight jog right)
9.7	right on Adanac St
10.0	right on Commercial Dr. *before* stop sign; 831 on right: Green Party office
10.1	1697 on right: Uprising Breads for great empanadas, but they're better known for their wholesome bread, whose heavenly aroma wafts about in the evening; other goodies include a variety of muffins and scones; since it's a collective, everyone who works there takes home a share of the profits and has a say in decision making; indoor seating; Mon-Fri 8:30 am-5:30 pm, Sat 9 am-5:30 pm, Sun closed; turn left

10.2 right on Commercial Dr. (Route V9)

10.6 1303 on right: San Marcos Bakery, everything from cinnamon doughnuts, strudels, cookies, and muffins to El Salvadorean specialties such as semitas, Maria Luisas, novias, and empanadas; 8 am-8 pm every day

11.0 cross busy 1st Ave

11.8 cross Broadway; a few doors west at 1638 E Broadway is Not Just Desserts; desserts with names such as Sin City, Peaches and Cream, Pumpkin Praline Cheesecake, Jumbleberry Pie — each comes on an elegantly garnished plate; indoor seating; Fri-Sat 11 am-2 pm, Sun-Thu 11 am-midnight; continue on Commercial Dr.

12.1 cross E 12th Ave

12.8 bear right on old part of Commercial Dr.

13.2 left on E 22nd Ave

13.4 right on Victoria Dr.

15.3 5658 on left: Greek Bakery (cross with care); tiny front area stocked with pita bread, baklava, and other Greek delicacies, Mon-Sat 9-6, Sun 10-5; 5752 on left: Venezia Ice Cream Mfg. Ltd, a wealth of natural flavours, Tues 9-6, Mon-Sat, Sun 2-6, closed Hol, indoor seating

15.6 right on E 43rd Ave

15.8 small open park on left

16.0 left on Argyle St

17.2 right into alley which becomes E 54th Ave, **caution:** unsigned intersections ahead

17.6 Knight St; **Caution: *poor visibility to left***

18.6 7007 Fraser St: Wonder Bakery is recommended for its raisin rounds — a filled two-layer cookie — but also has a good selection of cookies (some with chocolate coating) apple pastries, cakes, etc.; no seating; Mon-Sat 8 am-6 pm, Fri 8 am-6:30 pm; jog right to continue on E 54th Ave

19.1 right on Prince Edward St; some grass and benches around the Sunset Pk Rec. Centre (Route V7)

22.1 cross E King Edward Ave; **Caution: *unsigned intersections ahead***

23.2 left on E 14th Ave

24.6 reach Cambie St; 3086 Cambie (near E 15th Ave): Amy's Cake Shop specializes in luscious cream cakes, open daily 11 am-7 pm; cross Cambie St and continue W on E 14th Ave

A crisp fall day is ideal for the bakery tour.

24.9 right on Heather St; after 12th Ave it becomes a little rough, cracked, and bumpy

25.3 left on W 10th Ave

25.8 cross Oak St

26.5 cross Hemlock St (a little busy)

26.7 cross Granville St; 2567 Granville: Van den Bosch Patisserie Belge & Bakery, where everything looks scrumptious and they pride themselves on natural ingredients and pure imported Belgian chocolate, also great for pastries; closed Sun, Mon-Fri 8-6, Sat 9-5

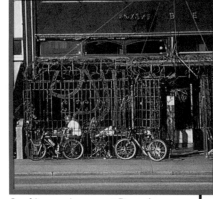

Locking-up is easy at Benny's.

28.4 right on Larch St

28.5 cross Broadway; just to left at 2505 W Broadway: Benny's Bagels and Pretzel Works Inc. with its unusual wrought iron-and-wood decor, great bagels (and generous portions of cream cheese), delicious cakes; indoor/outdoor seating, open 24 hours

28.6 left on W 8th Ave (Route V6)

30.5 left on Highbury St

30.7 left on W 10th **(use care)**; 3788 W 10th on right: A Piece of Cake has great cakes, cheesecakes, muffins, and pies; seating; Mon 7 am-12 am, Tue-Fri 7:30 am-12 am, Sat 8:30 am-10 pm, Sun 9 am-10 pm

30.8 left on Alma **(use care)** (Route V5)

31.3 right on W 5th Ave

33.3 left on Vine St

33.4 right on W 4th Ave (busier)

33.5 2242 on right (2/3 of way down from Vine to Yew): Forrester Bakery Ltd has excellent blueberry scones, positively mouth-watering yummy-looking cinnamon swirls and twists, cookies, etc. Mon-Fri 9:30 am-6 pm, Sat 9 am-5:30 pm

33.7 2142 on right (mid-block): Antonio Bakery has pies, tea buns, shortbread, etc.; seating; opens early! Mon-Fri 6 am-6:30 pm, Sat 7 am-6 pm, Sun 10:30 am-5 pm

34.0 1962 W 4th Ave on right (halfway between Maple and Cypress): au Chocolate features tasty little truffles, fresh-dipped Kits bars in several thick luscious flavours — milk, nut, dark dips, mint, chocolate, nut and vanilla centres, and desserts; if you're not paying attention, the elegant decor of this place could leave you thinking it's an antique furniture store; some seating; Mon-Sat noon-6 pm

34.1 left on Cypress St **(use care)**; bumpy ahead

34.6 cross Cornwall; last chances! 1833 Cornwall on right: Siegel's Bagels Ltd; watch nine varieties of Montreal-style bagels pour out of the 25 tonne wood-burning brick oven; indoor/outdoor seating; Mon-Sat 7 am-9:30 pm, Sun/Hol 7 am-8 pm; 1925 Cornwall on left: Frogurt's Cafe features hard and soft natural-flavoured yoghurt (get it in the homemade waffle cone); indoor/outdoor seating; Mon-Wed 10 am-11 pm, Thu-Sun 10 am-11:30 pm (and if you're still hungry, there's some of the best pizza in town a couple doors over at Flying Wedge Pizza!) **Caution: *unsigned intersections ahead***

35.1   right on Ogden at Maritime Museum (totem pole)

35.2   left on Chestnut St

35.2   end of route at end of Chestnut St

Do you eat to ride, or ride to eat? Either way, there's nothing like carbohydrates to keep those muscles energized, and if you're looking for a change from potatoes and pasta, this ride's for you. It takes you past a sampling of Vancouver's choice treat outlets. As this is a snacking tour, it bypasses the regular cafes and restaurants, to stop instead at bakeries and certain other specialty shops.

Sometimes one serving just won't do.

You'll find bakeries concentrated wherever people go for their grocery shopping — on West 4th Avenue, on East Hastings Street, on Denman Street, in Chinatown, and in Kerrisdale — but if there was a prize for the Vancouver street with the most bakeries within a 20 block stretch, it would probably go to the section of Commercial Drive south of Venables Street and north of 13th Avenue (though West Broadway would be a strong rival). Even though this tour doesn't take in all these areas, nevertheless be sure to pace yourself and don't plan on stopping at every single one of the over 20 places described or mentioned unless you're very, very hungry. However, if you are endowed with a great appetite, watch for other unmentioned bakeries en route.

In many of these establishments seating may be limited or nonexistent, but this gives you an excuse to retire to a nearby park. Since it's always more fun to eat with friends, get the gang together and enjoy!

RIGHT: Family cycling is a sharing affair.

NORTH & WEST VANCOUVER

The North Shore rises abruptly from Burrard Inlet to mountain peaks in the 1400 m range. Clear mountain streams cascade into deep canyons as they descend to the sea. Well-established second-growth conifers—and a few stands of old-growth-keep the slopes green year-round, except when cloaked in winter snow.

By keeping to the lower parts, you can follow the waterfront, with opportunities for swimming and beach exploration. Even down here, expect to climb a few hills, though; and the higher you go, the better the views. If you continue above the urban development into the area's provincial parks, you'll find several designated mountain-biking trails.

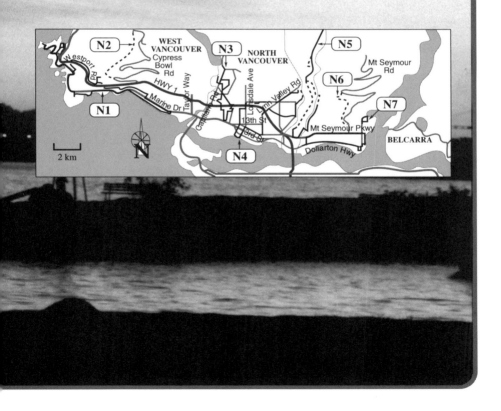

N1 • West Vancouver Shoreline

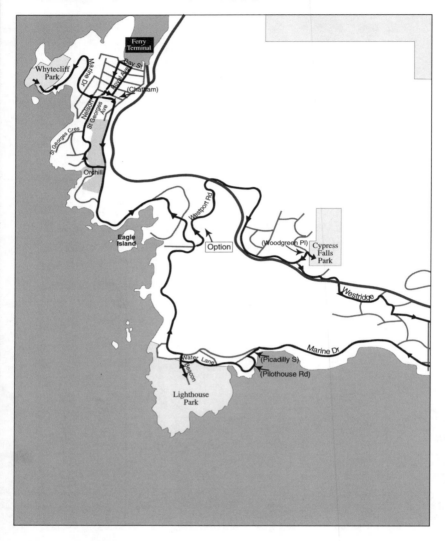

Distance & Elev Gain	36.6 km, 650 m or 38.4 km, 850 m; return
Terrain, Road, Traffic	rolling hills, steep in places; paved, with short stretches of gravel path; much on quiet streets, but take note that Marine Dr. is in places narrow and can be busy
Difficulty	F4/F5 T4
Bike	low gears, esp. for option
Access	W on Marine Dr. 1.2 km past Taylor Way, left on 13th St; or steeply down at end of Lions Gate Bridge and W on

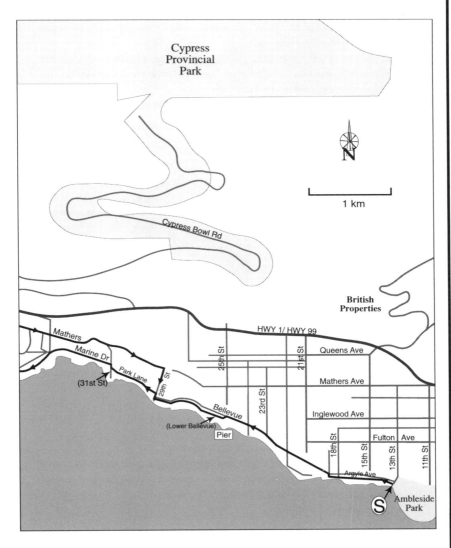

road to cross over Capilano R. to Park Royal Shopping Ctre and take trail to left downriver into E end of Ambleside Pk (also accessible from Welch St)

Short Description along the shore of West Vancouver from Ambleside to Horseshoe Bay, discovering promenades, historic sites, old-growth forest, a lighthouse, and rocky beaches, with an option to visit a waterfall

ROAD LOG

0.0 Argyle Ave at foot of 13th St, W end of Ambleside Pk; head W (note the occasional green and white bike route signs)

0.2 141 on left: Ferry Building Gallery, former ticket office, 12-8 pm, exc. Mon; pier

0.4 Ambleside-by-the-Sea Demonstration Compost Garden on left at 15th St;

0.6 John Lawson Pk: washrooms, picnic areas, pier

0.7 1768 on left: *Hollyburn House*, 1889 (unpainted wood duplex)

0.8 straight past 18th St on narrow gravel path

0.9 right on 19th St

1.0 left on Bellevue Ave

2.3 pass 24th St; one block N in Dundarave, Capers is at 25th St on S side

2.5 left over tracks and right on Lower Bellevue Ave; below are Dundarave Pk and pier, and Peppi's Restaurant (built in 1912 as *The Clachan* — Welsh for "meeting place"

3.5 right on 29th St

3.6 left on Park Lane (becomes Procter Ave)

4.2 right on 31st St

4.3 left on Marine Dr. (busier, somewhat narrow in places)

5.2 **Caution: *hidden intersection at Creery Ave***

8.1 angle left on Picadilly S; park access on left

Whytecliff Isle beckons to be explored.

8.4 left on Dogwood Lane/ Pilothouse Rd, passing park

8.7 memorial anchor to Francis William Caulfield on left

9.1 keep left to rejoin Picadilly S; Caulfeild Cove on left; 4773 on right: St Francis in the Wood Anglican Church

9.2 left on Water Lane, quite steep climbing, then down

9.8 left on Beacon Lane to enter Lighthouse Pk; note bike lockup rails at trail heads

10.2 end of parking lot gate; walk down main road to reach 1912 lighthouse (not open to public); head back N on Beacon Lane

10.7 left on Marine Dr.

12.5 Westport Rd and Eagle Harbour Community Ctre on right (note for return option)

13.6 Eagle Harbour

15.4 left on Orchill Rd, past Gleneagles Golf Course

15.6 keep right on St Georges Ave, fairly steep climb, then bear right passing St Georges Cres.

16.1 angle right as Nelson Ave takes over

16.3 left on Marine Dr.; **Caution: *watch for rocks***

18.1 left into Whytecliff Pk

18.4 road ends past horseshoe-shaped parking lot; gazebo and lookout just beyond; beach and washrooms are further around to S

18.9	right on Marine Dr.
20.7	left on Nelson Ave
20.9	right on Chatham St
21.0	left on Royal Ave
21.4	left on Bay St; Horseshoe Bay: ferry dock 0.2 km to right (to Bowen Island, Sunshine Coast, Vancouver Island), Sewell's Marina and waterfront park ahead
21.6	left on Nelson Ave
22.2	left on Marine Dr.
22.5	right on Marine Dr. to parallel Hwy 1; follow Marine Dr. and detour on Bellevue Ave at 31st St to finish at 13th St (36.6 km); or proceed as below **Option:** lilac climb to Cypress Falls
26.0	left on Westport Rd at Eagle Harbour Community Ctre, keep left passing Greenleaf Rd; quite steep in places
27.5	pass under Upper Levels/Hwy 99/Hwy 1
28.0	views available at small quarry on right
28.4	opposite Westwood Dr. look down to right for bird's-eye view of a razed-hilltop style housing development all too common lately
29.4	pass Woodcrest Rd on right (note for later); now on Woodgreen Dr.
29.6	right on Woodgreen Pl.
29.7	end of pavement, Cypress Falls Pk; continue straight on gravel road or across sports field to find walking trail upstream through woods past two cascades and several groves of huge Douglas firs; **return same way**
30.0	left on Woodgreen Dr.
30.2	left on Woodcrest Rd
30.5	right on Almondel Rd
30.9	under Hwy 1/Hwy 99
31.1	becomes Ripple Rd, straight past Ripple Pl.
31.4	left on Westridge Ave
31.8	right on Southridge Ave
32.4	right on Bayridge Ave
32.6	left on Mathers Ave at McKechnie Pk, "no exit," steepish descent
32.8	straight on 0.1 km crushed limestone path
33.9	straight on Mathers Ave at 31st St
34.7	right on 29th St
34.9	left on Marine Dr., or continue 0.2 km and left on Bellevue Ave
38.4	back at 13th St, Ambleside Pk (slightly more if you took Bellevue Ave) **More information:** *Hiking Guide to the Big Trees* by Randy Stoltmann

Ambleside Park, long a popular place for picnicking and beach activities, is the starting point for this ride. Almost immediately, you pass the former ferry ticket office and waiting room, opened in 1913. The end of wartime gas rationing, and increased use of automobiles on new roads and on the 1938 Lion's Gate Bridge, contributed to its closure in 1947; it was thereafter for many years a municipal transit office. Nearby is the oldest house in West Vancouver, the 1889 *Hollyburn House*. Here lived John "Navvy Jack" Lawson, captain of the first ferry service, which ran from 1866 to 1867.

Attractive waterfront apartment buildings let you pretend briefly that you're in Honolulu, then you can head up to Marine Drive to experience the more British flavour of Dundarave. Among its highlights is Capers, a popular health food store and stylish restaurant. Back at the waterfront is Dundarave Park. The pier was built in response to residents' demands for ferry service. Because not enough people used it, the ferry was replaced in 1916 by a bus to Ambleside. The pier became popular for recreation.

Pleasant rural roads finally run out, leaving Marine Drive as your only choice — a not wholly unpleasant prospect, however. Soon you once again detour onto quieter roads, passing a largely undeveloped shore-front park where blackberries grow wonderfully sweet in the August heat. Further along are picturesque little Caulfeild Cove and sturdy but graceful St Francis in the Wood Anglican Church. A short but steep up-and-over brings you to Lighthouse Park.

Flowerbeds brighten Marine Drive in Ambleside.

Since 1875 the Point Atkinson lighthouse at the tip of the park has warned ships to steer clear of the rocky shore. The establishment of a 75 ha lighthouse reserve in 1881 has likewise directed loggers and developers elsewhere, leaving this as the last remaining stand of virgin timber in the Lower Mainland.

Beyond crowded Eagle Harbour you ride right along the shore, and then on less-used roads, to arrive at Whytecliff Park. It's a fine place to picnic. For more of an adventure, clamber along the rock causeway to explore the small island just offshore — if you don't mind getting a little wet. To continue on to the restaurant-rich ferry departure point of Horseshoe Bay, you'll have to backtrack; unfortunately there are no other options.

You may return via (almost) the same route or wholly on Marine Drive, but if you feel like more exercise, take the lilac-trimmed alternative up to the picturesque waterfalls and tall trees at Cypress Falls Park. This latter return option takes quieter residential roads almost as far as Dundarave.

RIGHT: The hiking trails at Cypress Falls are a refreshing counterpoint to cycling.

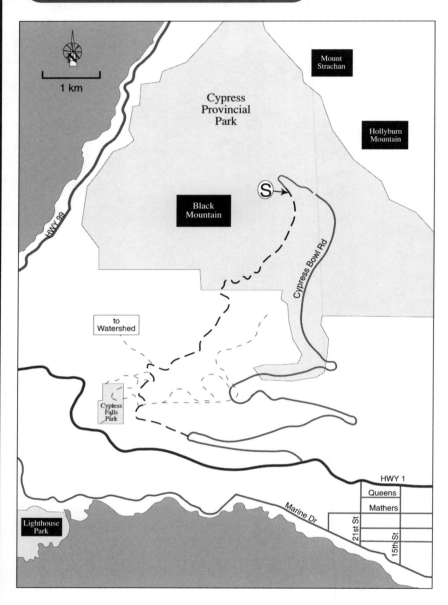

Distance and Elev Gain 7.8 km, (650 m), one way

Terrain, Road, Traffic from level to quite steep; mostly coarse gravel to rocky, though bottom 2 km are fairly smooth, snow and ice likely from mid fall to early summer; service vehicles on rare occasions

Difficulty F5 T1

Bike mountain bike with fat knobby tires, low gears, and good brakes

Access leave Hwy 99/Hwy 1/Upper Levels 4 km W of W. Vancouver's Taylor Way at Exit 8 to take Cypress Parkway; the bottom end of the trail is at 2.2 km, just beyond Quarry Lookout, on the outside of the first switchback; to reach the top end, remain on the main road and continue to the end of the downhill ski parking lot, at 15.5 km; the ride up is typically a 5-10% grade with two lanes and makes for good road bike training too, low-moderate traffic (watch for recessed gratings and occasional loose rock)

Short Description "at your own risk" mountain biking trail, a rocky, steepish ride to and/or from 900 m elevation, with small creeks, views, alder thickets, established second-growth, and huckle-, black-, and blueberries

---

ROAD LOG

Notes: food, drink, and washrooms available at downhill skiing parking area; watch for other riders and hikers

0.0 end of downhill skiing parking lot; head S on gravel trail past yellow gate; quite steeply down

0.2 first of two switchbacks, then less steep

0.6 keep right at bare rock

1.1 three stream crossings over next 0.7 km

2.0 slight uphill

2.3 curving to right and back, views

2.7 cross rocky creek bed

2.8 descend again

3.1 older second-growth begins

3.2 two-log bridge with culvert

3.3 abandoned quarry, fairly steep descent

3.5 switchback turn to left, then curving back to right, less steep

4.1 steeper

4.2 curve right

4.4 descend moderately steeply through intermittent thickets of alders

4.9 small waterfall on right, culvert

5.4 steeper, rougher section

5.5 smoother, small zigzag

5.7 crushed limestone/pavement begins, "watershed" posted on paved road on right

5.9 curves left, then right

Heading up the gentler lower reaches of the BLT.

6.3	pass turnoff to Cypress Falls, W side, on right, then bridge
6.6	BC Hydro substation
6.7	Cypress Falls trail, E side, on right
6.8	**Caution:** *first of several water bars across road; then curve left and fairly steep*
7.4	quarry on right
7.8	gate and Cypress Parkway
	More information: BC Parks office: 929-4818

The BLT trail on the flank of Black Mountain is one of the few officially recognized mountain biking trails in the Vancouver area. Since its upper and lower halves are so different, it can cater to mountain bikers with either developing or established skills. Over its lower 2 km the trail is smoother, generally wider, and less steep, while higher up it is better suited to the more adventurous rider, though it is not especially technical. Here it earns its name, for BLT stands for Boulders, Logs, and Trees. In truth it's mostly the steepness and the rocks that you have to watch out for, unless you are so unfortunate as to either leave the trail to collide with logs or trees, or unexpectedly find one fallen across your path.

The upper end of the BLT: climb aboard and hold on.

Depending on your abilities and inclinations, you can choose either to enter at the bottom end, ride as far you want (perhaps to the top), then return via the same route, or to take the road to the top end and ride the trail down. The former is perhaps the safest, because you will see at your leisure on the way up the hazards you will confront again on the way down at greater speed, but it is also more physically demanding. (The route is described from the top down, because the odometer seems a little more accurate in this direction.) Whether you arrive at the top via the road or the trail, if it's late summer, be sure to scour the roadsides and/or ski slopes for luscious wild blueberries.

From the trail's beginning at the end of the downhill skiing parking area, you are immediately challenged by a steep, switchbacking descent, on chunky gravel, through brushy surroundings. Although the trail smooths out at times, the rocks otherwise tend to vary between walnut and fist size, with a sprinkling of grapefruit-to-breadbox sized specimens for good measure. Here and there a stream crosses the old logging road. The trail levels out for a bit, then you descend again, into established forest.

After several curves, you find yourself passing through intermittent thickets of close-set young alders, at whose bases tiny evergreens plot their eventual overthrow. As usual, just when you think the jarring is over, you'll once again find yourself bounced playfully from rock to rock. Perhaps some alarmed squirrel will take time out from seed gathering to scold you for your intrusion.

By and by, your going really does get easier, as the way turns to crushed limestone alternating with pavement. Turnoffs for Cypress Falls appear (not really cycling trails, though), and you pass a BC Hydro substation. Through this disturbed landscape you encounter occasional blackberry patches, then you reach the Cypress Parkway.

Logging on Black Mountain began around 1899, so the conifers have had time to grow back in places where enough soil remained. Elsewhere, however, you will find nothing but scrubby bushes and dense thickets of young alder growing among the rocks. It will take many, many years before these latter areas are once again forested in Douglas firs and red cedars as grand as those that previously stood here.

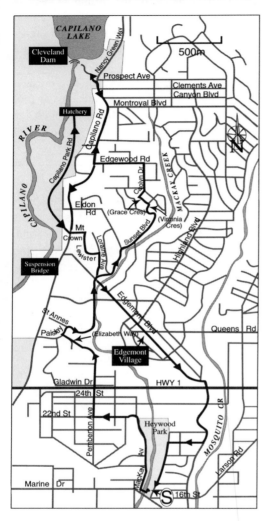

Distance and Elev Gain	13.8 km, 225 m, return
Terrain, Road, Traffic	mostly uphill followed by mostly downhill, mostly gently to moderately steep; paved with about 0.2 km gravel trail; mostly low traffic, busier on Edgemont Blvd and Capilano Rd
Difficulty	F3 T4
Bike	gears recommended
Access	take Marine Dr. to 16th St and go 0.1 km N on Hamilton Ave and left into Heywood Pk (across from Capilano Mall, City of North Vancouver)

Short Description   a trip to Capilano Canyon to enjoy the forest and river,
see the dam that collects much of Greater Vancouver's
drinking water behind it, and visit a fish hatchery with
interpretive displays

ROAD LOG

0.0   Heywood Pk, by gate at N end of parking lot; go N on crushed limestone path, then left across Mackay Creek to head SW (use care, watch for pedestrians)

0.1   right on Mackay Ave (about 0.1 km above Marine Dr.) to climb fairly steeply

0.8   curve left on 22nd St

1.2   right on Pemberton Ave

1.4   cross 24th St/Plateau Dr. onto gravel trail and overpass crossing Hwy 99/Hwy 1

1.6   cross Gladwin Dr. to continue N on Pemberton Ave

1.9   continue on gravel and take left fork, becomes paved at tennis courts

2.1   right on Elizabeth Way

2.2   right on Paisley Rd

2.3   keep right on Paisley Rd at St Anne's Dr.

3.1   cross Edgemont Dr. and bear right on Sunset Blvd

3.9   right on Virginia Cres. just past sharp curve to left

4.1   fork left on Grace Cres.

4.2   continue N on Carolyn Dr.

4.5   left on Edgewood Rd

4.9   right on Capilano Rd

5.5   keep left past Montroyal Blvd

*Massive stumps near the hatchery bear
slots for the loggers' springboards.*

5.8   cross (with care) at bend to gated access road to Cleveland Dam/Capilano River Regional Pk; continue on foot within park or take Capilano Rd back S (downhill, curving) after touring dam surroundings

7.4   Capilano Pk Road on right leads to fish hatchery (best Jul-Oct); **Caution: *use extreme care, taking into account the descent leading to it, the sharpness of the turn, and the"no right turn" sign*** (**Note:** The option of making a left turn from a northbound approach and then continuing with another left turn on Capilano is no more attractive a prospect for many cyclists. The GVRD and North Vancouver District could probably do better.); stay on main road to pass the "buses only" sign (note special trees mentioned in text)

8.8   arrive at hatchery; **retrace route**

10.3   cross Capilano Rd to Mt Crown Rd (curves into Lewister Rd); (use care, consider walking instead of riding); or for Capilano Suspension Bridge (3735 Capilano Rd, 985-7474) go 0.4 km further S; afterwards backtrack a little and go SE on Edgemont Blvd

10.7   right on Loraine Ave

11.0   right on Sunset Dr., left on Edgemont Blvd

More information: GVRD Parks: 224-5739.

Hiking Guide to the Big Trees by Randy Stoltmann

In *Legends of Vancouver*, Pauline Johnson calls the Capilano "that purest, most restless river in all Canada . . . haunted with tradition, teeming with a score of romances that vie with its grandeur and loveliness, and of which its waters are perpetually whispering." It is still a lovely river, though since 1889 these vital waters have been harnessed for use by the good citizens of Greater Vancouver via a pipeline beneath Burrard Inlet.

As the lower part of Capilano Road doesn't make for very pleasant cycling, a more appealing approach has been devised. Beginning at attractive Heywood Park, you follow quiet residential roads and trails up along Mackay Creek, much of it in a wooded setting. Eventually you do join Capilano Road where traffic is thinner, and soon reach the massive Cleveland Dam. (You can continue 3.2 km further and 150 m higher to the Grouse Mountain Skyride at the end of Nancy Greene Way — but don't expect to bring your bike up the mountain.)

Walk out on top of the 90 m high dam to see the 75 billion litre lake behind it or look down into the steep canyon on the other side. Trails and viewpoints allow different vantage points of both the dam and the canyon. Unfortunately, hardly any trails within the park have been opened to cyclists; it is suggested that you proceed on foot, with your bike or with it securely locked up. You can find your way through the park to the hatchery if you wish, or take the (not quite satisfactory) road route described. At the north end of the hatchery parking lot, note the exceptionally tall (77 m) Douglas fir. Nearby, at the southwestern edge of the bus loop, are Pacific yew (the species in whose bark taxol, a promising anti-cancer drug, was found).

Live salmon, trout, and other fish are on display at the hatchery. Artificial specimens are exhibited as well so you can learn their various markings. Rounding out the facility are a fish ladder, rearing ponds, and a gift shop.

If you have the inclination to visit the Capilano Suspension Bridge, a commercial attraction since the beginning of the 20th century, you may do so with a slight detour. (Be advised, however, that there is a free suspension bridge across Lynn Canyon, albeit in humbler company, without the native carvings—see route N4.) The return leg of the route, which passes through pretty Edgemont Village, is fairly straightforward and mostly downhill.

RIGHT: A stop at the bakery in Edgemont Village helps round out the ride.

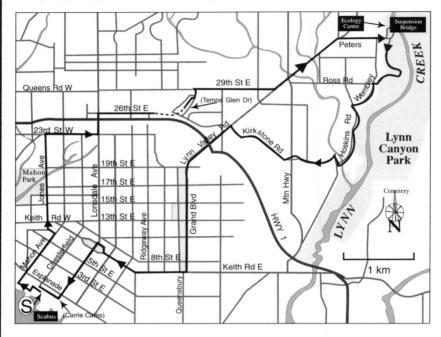

Distance and Elev Gain 17.4 km, 275 m, return

Terrain, Road, Traffic mostly uphill going and downhill (with one steepish climb) on the return; largely paved roads, with a short stretch on a trail and 1 km on gravel road; low-moderate traffic roads with the exception of the 3.9 km along busier 23rd St, Lonsdale Ave, and Lynn Valley Rd

Difficulty F4 T4

Bike any bike with good climbing ability and brakes

Access Seabus from Vancouver or from Esplanade in N. Vancouver

Short Description from the waterfront up to the base of the mountains, to visit an ecology centre and a suspension bridge over a deep whitewater creek canyon in a forested park

---

ROAD LOG

0.0 E end of Chadwick Court loop at foot of Chesterfield Ave, immediately W of Seabus Terminal; head W

0.1 cross Chesterfield Ave onto red paver lane, "no thoroughfare"

0.2 left at red buoy to head S past washrooms towards covered lookout, then right to follow shoreline

0.3 continue past Sailors' Point

0.4 right on lane (St Paul's to left), passing gate and crossing Esplanade **(use care)** to continue (uphill) on Mahon Ave

0.7 cross 1st St **(divided, use care)**

0.9 cross 3rd St; option to detour right on 3rd St,through alley, or on 4th St to North Shore Museum and Archives at 209 W 4th St, free, open Wed-Sun 1-4 pm, archives 9:30 am-12:30 pm and 1:30-4:30 pm, 987-5618; in same building is Presentation Gallery at 333 Chesterfield; month-long photographic exhibitions in (remodelled) 1902 North Vancouver School, $2, Wed-Sun 12-5 pm (Thu to 9 pm), 986-1351; behind, along 3rd, is Anne MacDonald Hall, the 1899 Church of St John the Evangelist

1.3 left on 6th St, then keep right at fork and right on Jones Ave

1.4 cross divided Keith Rd **(use care)**

1.8 Mahon Pk on left

2.6 right on 23rd St W

3.2 left on Lonsdale Ave **(use care)**

3.6 right on 26th St E

4.3 cross Ridgeway Ave, ignore "no exit"

4.5 road ends; angle left on short, narrow hogfuel trail to lane; follow lane

4.9 left on Tempe Glen Dr.

5.0 right on 29th St

5.9 left on Lynn Valley Rd; shopping mall

7.1 right on Peters Rd

7.8 left to enter Lynn Canyon Pk, 6 am-10 pm

7.9 Lynn Canyon Ecology Centre on left, free, 10 am-5 pm daily, closed weekends in Dec-Jan (987-5922)

8.0 washrooms and bike rack on right, concession stand on left; access to suspension bridge is just beyond on left (warning: though pools in the canyon were once used for swimming, the death toll for the past decade has averaged over one per year (caused by falling rocks, diving onto rocks, etc.); access is now fenced off in the interests of public safety); continue E on road and curve right to follow edge of canyon

8.2 turn left (gravel) instead of heading out on Peters Rd

9.2 pavement resumes; then begin Ross Rd at Duval Rd

9.4 left on Wembley Dr.

9.9 left on Hoskins Rd

10.2 fairly steep descent, views across to Alberta Wheat Pool

10.7 cross Hastings Creek

10.8 right on Arborlynn Dr.

11.0 curve left on 20th St, moderately steep uphill

11.6 cross Mountain Hwy, continue on Kirkstone Rd

12.0 Kirkstone Pk on right

12.5 left on Lynn Valley Rd

12.9 straight; watch out for freeway-bound traffic

13.3	straight on Grand Blvd, past a half-block wide park on the right from 19th to Keith Rd
14.7	right on Keith Rd
15.8	divided Keith Rd widens to make room for pretty Victoria Pk
16.0	left on Lonsdale Ave; moderate downhill
16.5	beyond 3rd St is the older section of town
16.8	93 on right: Woodlands Natural Food Restaurant; 90 on left: Paine Hardware in Aberdeen Block
17.0	curve right on Carrie Cates Cres.; continue straight, or walk along outside of Lonsdale Quay back to start
17.2	left on Chesterfield Ave and left again on Chadwick Pl.
17.4	back at start

North Vancouver was initially seen by the white settlers only as a source of timber. The first sawmill was set up in the early 1860s. Under the subsequent ownership of Sewell Prescott Moody, it thrived as Burrard Inlet Lumber Mills. The surrounding townsite became known as Moodyville. The mill fell idle, burning in 1916, but by this time the settlement had already withered, deposed by the one growing up 1.5 km to the west at the foot of Lonsdale Avenue. Today nothing remains of Moodyville, but some buildings from early times remain along lower Lonsdale Avenue; one notable business is Paine Hardware, which dates from 1908.

Savour the rugged splendor of Lynn Canyon from mid-span.

Ironically, the beginning of Seabus operations in 1976 simply reinstated a ferry service discontinued 18 years earlier after nearly a century of operation. Rather than build another crossing to handle the growing number of cars choking the bridges during peak periods, planning authorities decided it made more sense to accommodate commuters on public transit instead. Adjacent to the Seabus terminal is Lonsdale Quay, a large structure enclosing a marketplace, shops, and restaurants.

You begin this ride by travelling through a waterfront park area. Among its highlights are a lookout giving views of Burrard Inlet and the Vancouver skyline, and Sailors' Point, dedicated in recognition of local maritime history. As you turn north, look to your left to see St Paul's, the oldest surviving mission church in the Vancouver area, dating from 1884 (restored 1983). For a break on the way uphill, take a detour to the North Shore Museum, with its changing displays, and Presentation Gallery, for photographic exhibitions.

Continuing up the slope and then eastward (sneakily avoiding unnecessary climbing) you reach Lynn Valley Road. In earlier days, this area was served by a BC Electric Railway streetcar line from the waterfront. From here Lynn Canyon Park is within easy reach.

Lynn Canyon Ecology Centre, at the entrance to the park, is a good choice for interpretive displays of all sorts, wildlife films, and weekend guided nature walks. The centre is also very active in school and community programs involving nature lore, bird counts, habitat conservation, recycling, storm drain marking, etc.

The existence of Lynn Canyon Park is due to the enterprising J.P. Crawford, a district councillor and land agent. In 1910 he persuaded the McTavish brothers of Vancouver, his clients, to donate about 5 ha to the district as a park to enhance the value of the rest of their land. An additional 4 ha were soon purchased. Councillor Crawford then built his house at the top of a steep trail leading to the park and set up a refreshment stand to catch thirsty patrons on their way out. He also dreamt up the idea of a suspension bridge overlooking the impressive canyon, doubtless inspired by the one on the Capilano. Although this bridge too began as a money-making enterprise, the district eventually acquired and repaired it, reopening it toll-free. It remains a popular attraction, as does the heavily forested park, since further enlarged.

A jarring ride not to be attempted if the bridge is occupied.

Winding pleasantly along through the park, you eventually return to residential streets. Most of the way back is flat or downhill, but there is one challenging slope to climb. As you coast downhill, be sure to take in the views across the water.

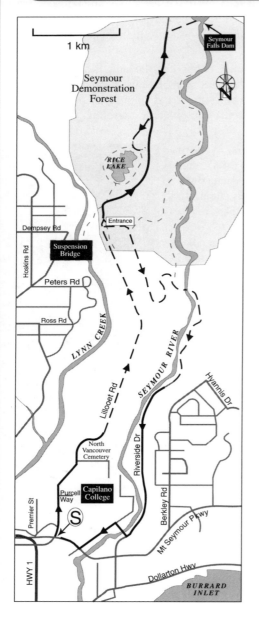

Distance and Elev Gain complete: 35.4 km, 475 m, return; (entrance area to dam and hatchery 23.3 km, 275 m, return)

Terrain, Road, Traffic flat to rolling hills; 1.8 km on narrow dirt path, 8.3 km on gravel roads and tracks, 25 km on pavement; no or little

traffic except for two short sections on
Mt Seymour Parkway and Lillooet Rd.

Difficulty complete: F4 T3 (from entrance area: F3 T1)

Bike complete: mountain bike recommended
(from entrance area: any bike)

Access take Keith Rd to Mountain Hwy and go S 0.2 km
(or 0.7 km N from Cotton Dr./Main St) then cross
Hwy 1/Hwy 99 on Fern St overpass; or, from Dollarton
Hwy go 0.4 km N on Riverside Dr., then go 0.8 km W; or,
by car only: take Hwy 1 Exit 22 (0.8 km N of Second
Narrows Bridge); park near Capilano College, or at
demonstration forest entrance area (Route N7)

Short Description getting away from it all in a demonstration forest, you can
visit a dam and feed the fish at a hatchery

ROAD LOG

0.0 Lillooet Rd at Seymour Parkway; go N

0.6 pass Purcell Way, access to Capilano College

0.8 1301 on left: equestrian centre

1.2 North Vancouver Cemetery

1.6 begin gravel (embankment trail is soft)

2.9 cross Baden Powell Trail

3.3 pass shooting range

4.6 paved

4.7 2.59 m dia., 653-year old Douglas
fir log

4.8 Seymour Demonstration Forest
entrance area: parking, gate,
drinking water (just beyond kiosk)
Optional starting point

7.0 weekday "no cycling beyond" point

9.5 S-curve, descent

9.8 pass spur bridge turnoff (no cycling
beyond river)

Hungry fish flash silver at feeding time.

10.2 right on Mid Valley Viewpoint
gravel access road, outhouses; continue N to rejoin main
road shortly

10.6 road from viewpoint merges

14.8 jog left then back

15.6 concrete bridge

15.7 bear right on gravel

15.8 bear left towards dam (fish hatchery to right), outhouses

16.0 base of dam; **retrace to fork**

16.3	left to fish hatchery
16.5	hatchery, bike racks; return to paved road to head back
16.9	concrete bridge
25.5	bear right at "no cycling beyond" point on good gravel track atop water main
26.6	left just past short incline at Rice Lake, keep left
26.9	right on main road
28.1	**Options:**
	1. end here
	2. retrace your route
	3. mountain bike route via Twin Bridges as described below left on gravel road just past main gate
28.4	right on gravel track beyond parking lot and gate
29.3	fairly steep descent
29.6	switchback left
30.4	fairly steep descent
30.5	cross Seymour River on N of twin bridges, right on far side on narrow, hard-packed dirt trail; occasional rougher and wetter spots
30.9	keep right/level at fork
31.0	creek crossing; just beyond is an old piece of wooden water pipe, held together with heavy steel wire wrap
31.3	pass steep trail up to left
31.8	keep right/level at fork
32.0	rocky section
32.1	partial washout (for 30 m) at small creek **(use care)**
32.3	straight on Riverside Dr., paved road, just past Baden Powell Trail and bridge
33.7	pleasant riverbank spot among the trees on right
34.4	sharp right on Grantham Rd
34.5	cross Seymour River
34.6	left on Seymour Boulevard, ignore "no exit" sign
35.1	right on Mt Seymour Pkwy beyond barriers
35.4	Lillooet Rd, end of route
	Site Information: 432-6286

There's a strip of smooth pavement here, almost 11 km long and wooded, and you don't have to compete with cars when you use it. The only potential drawbacks are that it's only open on weekends and that getting there involves negotiating 3 km of gravel road. This last point is not a problem if you've got a mountain bike, though. A lot of families drive to the start of the pavement, their cars bristling with bikes. Then everyone piles out and they set off at a leisurely pace, the smallest tots riding in bike trailers.

While you're cycling at the Seymour Demonstration Forest, you'll see examples of forest management and interpretation panels along the way. If you want to know more, pick up a pamphlet at the entrance to assist with the explanations. (Note that what you see here is not necessarily typical of what goes on in the rest of BC's woodlands.) There are still tracts of reasonably intact forest, giving many opportunities to sneak off on foot into the peace of the deep, dark woods for a while.

To get there, you begin by climbing up past an equestrian centre and Capilano College. Beyond the North Vancouver Cemetery, the road turns to fairly loose gravel. The road improves once you pass the shooting range, becoming paved just before the sheltered 653-year-old Douglas fir log.

The end of the road.

If you're a berry fancier, keep alert for salmon-, salal-, thimble- and red huckleberries. At Mid Valley Viewpoint you have a commanding view up and down the wooded valley of the Seymour River. While relaxing, try to pick out which areas have recently been logged, and what tree species you are seeing. Near this point in 1907 the first (rock) dam on the Seymour was built to supply water to Vancouver, supplementing the flow from the Capilano River. It was later rebuilt upstream.

As you approach the present dam, the thunder of the falling water becomes noticeable. Although it looks big, at 21 m it's less than one quarter the height of the Cleveland Dam on the Capilano. Nearby, at the hatchery, watch the fish-blackened ponds erupt in flashing silver at feeding time (or you can buy feed from dispensers and do it yourself).

Coming back, take the same road. Although there are various side trails, many are pedestrian-only. If gravel's not a problem, follow the pipeline where it branches off to Rice Lake, which might one day be attractive for swimming, then return to the main road. For a more challenging and largely car-free ending, turn left just past the entrance to head downhill on gravel. Cross the river at the best of the twin bridges and then follow a narrow, wooded (sometimes tricky) trail to the end of Riverside Drive. A few more turns and another river crossing bring you back to Mount Seymour Parkway, near your starting point.

N6 • *Old Buck Trail*

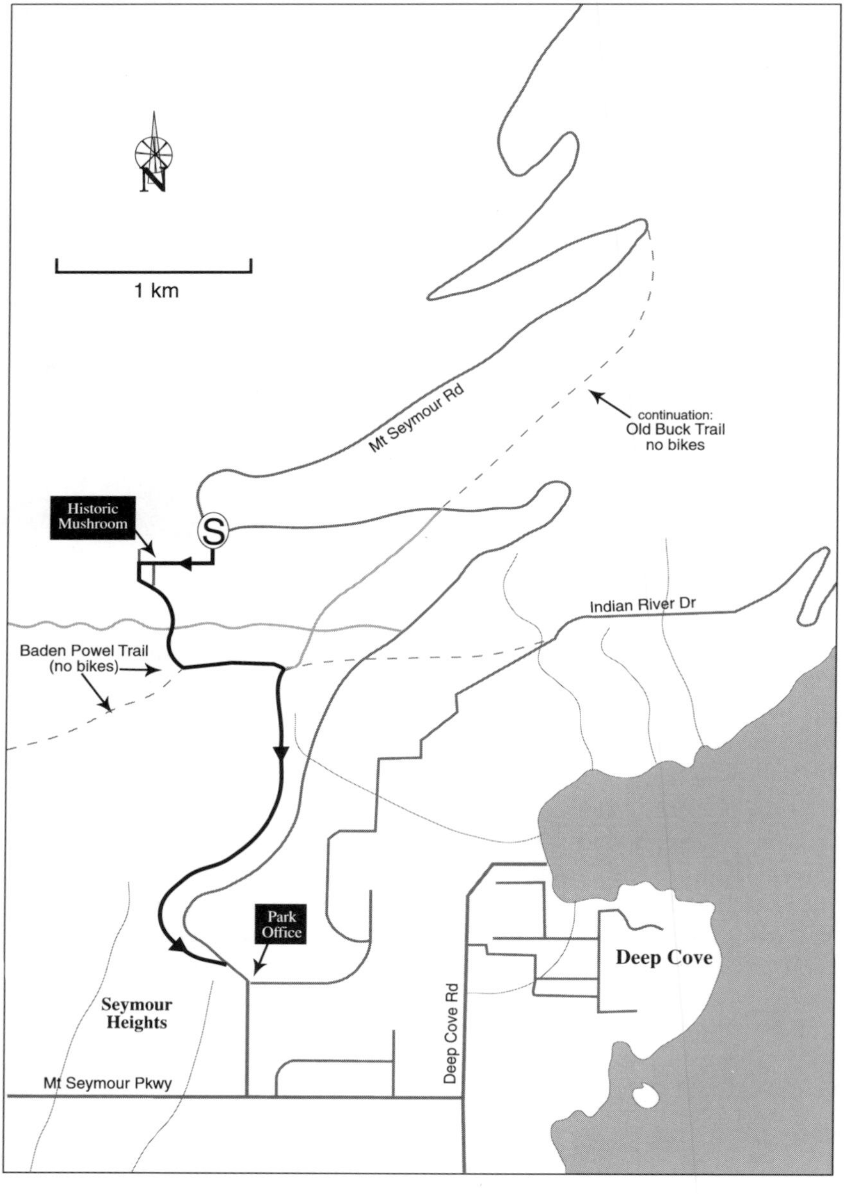
N
1 km
Mt Seymour Rd
continuation:
Old Buck Trail
no bikes
Historic
Mushroom
S
Indian River Dr
Baden Powel Trail
(no bikes)
Park
Office
Deep Cove
Seymour
Heights
Deep Cove Rd
Mt Seymour Pkwy

Distance and Elev Gain 4.5 km, (450 m), one way

Terrain, Road, Traffic moderate-to-steep grades; fairly bumpy dirt and rock trail, muddy in places, 0.8 to 1.5 m wide, snow and ice likely from late fall to late spring

Difficulty F5 T1

Bike mountain bike with low gears, good brakes, fat knobby tires

Access from Mt Seymour Pkwy 4.8 km E of Hwy 1/Hwy 99, head 0.6 km N on Indian River Dr., going straight on Mt Seymour Rd to find lower end of trail on left immediately beyond park gate; for upper end, keep going up the road (typ. 7-9% grade, 2 lanes up) 5.6 km for the steeper trail as described below (cross road at Vancouver Lookout picnic area — 5.4 km — and continue uphill behind barrier), or head left at 4.2 km for a less steep access point (Route N7)

Short Description "at your own risk" mountain bike trail, a short but challenging ride through the woods of Mt Seymour

---

ROAD LOG

0.0 Old Buck Access Trail on S side of Mt Seymour Rd just into second switchback; head S, steeply downhill

0.2 right, not straight, at bottom of slope

0.5 Historic Mushroom parking lot; keep straight past interpretive panel

0.6 left at the T ("unmarked trail" to right)

0.7 pass trail merging from left

1.1 cross small bridge and power line trail to re-enter woods

1.2 left to join Baden Powell Trail

1.3 rocky section, creek crossings, logs

1.7 bridge

1.8 intermittent stream bed

2.2 Caution: *three tire-trapping bridges, then bumpy again*

2.3 another tire catcher and stream crossing, bumpy

2.4 right on Old Buck Trail (go straight for uphill branch of Old Buck Trail), steepish and rocky, then steeper

2.7 stream crossing, rocks

2.8 smoother

2.9 take right fork

3.1 wet stretches for 0.6 km

3.4 stream

3.6 pass NSHA loop on right

3.9 near Mt Seymour Rd

4.0 cross small creek, no bridge, then crushed limestone and smooth

4.2 small bridge, NSHA loop on right

4.4 small raised bridge

4.5 trail ends at park gate

More information: BC Parks office: 929-4818

The Old Buck Trail is one of the few trails near Vancouver that has actually been designated for mountain biking. It largely follows a former logging road that, from its genesis in the 1920s until the construction of the Mt Seymour Road in the 1950s, was the only road up Mt Seymour. Many Vancouverites built weekend ski cabins on the mountain, which they would reach either by driving or taking the bus up this rather steep road to the Historic Mushroom parking lot and hiking from there. Ironically, the designation of the park in 1936, an event supported by the cabin owners, marked the decline of the sociable cabin era. In recent years, mountain bikers have volunteered their help in maintaining this trail, in coordination with BC Parks.

Unlike the BLT (see Route N2), the Old Buck Trail goes almost entirely through established second-growth coniferous forest, with a lot more dirt mixed in with the rocks. Like the BLT, however, this trail has its steepest parts uppermost, though you can avoid some of the most villainously so if you desire. The route is described from the top down to hopefully achieve more accurate measurements. Your options are to start from the bottom and grind your way up, or to take the paved road to the Vancouver Lookout (pause for the view), using the trail only for coming down. Either way, be especially alert for other trail users, ahead or approaching from behind.

The way down begins on a fiercely steep, needle-covered dirt trail through a forest of princely younger conifers growing amidst the stumps and fallen trunks of the ancient monarchs. Occasional exposed rocks make the ride a little rougher. There is a right angle turn, then the trail becomes tamer. Shortly you reach the Historic Mushroom parking lot. A decaying stump is all that remains of the famous rustic message centre from which the site got its name.

Having skirted the outside of the former parking lot, you descend anew, but at a less frantic rate. Crossing a small ditch brings you to the power line trail, bordered by periodically cut dense thickets of black cottonwood, alder, and willow. Following for a while the Baden Powell Trail, you encounter a trickier section that is rockier and involves several creek crossings. At times the stream actually makes its bed on the trail. Watch that you don't trap your tires on the next few bridges!

Parting from the Baden Powell Trail, the way is at first steep and rocky, then becomes for a while smoother but steeper. A prolonged stream crossing has you looking for the vestiges of a smooth trail along the edge of the rocks. Note the partially buried power cable. The trail is often really quite pleasant, and has obviously been painstakingly improved, yet it is still muddy much of the rest of the way down. Eventually, you come quite close to Mt Seymour Road and cross a small, unbridged creek. From here, the last little bit is easy going, but mind the raised bridges.

RIGHT: The road is a little easier but the trail is more interesting.

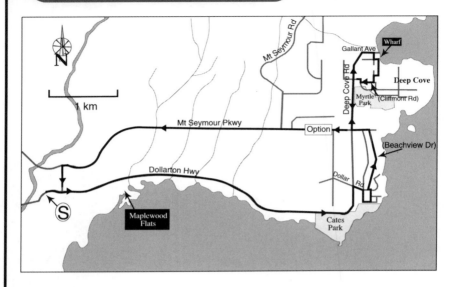

Distance and Elev Gain	17.5 km, 200 m (option: 16.6 km, 250 m) return
Terrain, Road, Traffic	gently rolling, but with several short steepish climbs in Dollarton/Deep Cove; paved roads; low traffic on side streets, but moderate traffic possible on Dollarton Hwy and on Mt Seymour Pkwy (2.8 km of bike lane)
Difficulty	F3 T4
Bike	gears recommended
Access	from Vancouver/Burnaby take Second Narrows Bridge and head 0.6 km E on Main St/Dollarton Hwy; from points W take Low Level Rd or 3rd St, and then Cotton Dr. and Main St, E beyond bridge to same point (if arriving by car, look for parking on left along Seymour River Place rather than in the more theft-prone industrial area on the right) (Routes N6, N5)
Short Description	a shoreline ride to Deep Cove that includes a proposed wildlife sanctuary, swimming and picnicking possibilities, picturesque views, and two fine examples of native carving

ROAD LOG

0.0 Dollarton Hwy at Seymour River Place (on left, small shopping mall on right); head E

0.8 2420 on left: Canadian International College

1.2 Maplewood Flats (proposed) Wildlife Sanctuary, just past chain link fence on right; main access trail begins beside the sign, perpendicular to the road

1.8 Burrard Inlet Indian Reserve

4.2	3919 on right: McKenzie Barge and Marineways
4.6	right into Cate's Pk; keep right to descend past boat launch and picnic areas
5.0	left opposite the concession/washrooms to exit (detour straight for totem and canoe)
5.2	left, then right on access road
5.4	right on Dollarton Hwy (becomes Deep Cove Rd)
6.0	right on Dollar Rd
6.1	right on Roslyn Blvd
6.3	curve left on Cates Pk Rd
6.5	end of road; Dollar Mill foundation ahead; return up the hill
6.6	right on Beachview Dr.
6.8	jog left to continue past Dollar Rd
7.8	left on Mt Seymour Pkwy
8.0	right on Deep Cove Rd
8.6	Myrtle Pk on right

Child-crank conversions let the young ones pedal along with mom or dad.

9.3	curve right on Gallant Ave towards downtown; 4310 on left: Deep Cove Bike Shop in converted garage, 10:30 am-6:30 pm, closed Mon (929-1918)
9.4	Panorama Dr. on left (half a block to a park/beach); for great honey-and-buttermilk doughnuts, try Honey Doughnuts and Goodies, just past Panorama Dr., at 4373 on the right
9.5	right on Banbury Rd at end of Gallant; viewing area, wharf, promenade, Deep Cove Pk
9.6	left on Naughton Ave (curves into Rockcliff Rd)
9.9	right on Raeburn St
10.0	left on Banbury Rd
10.1	right on Cliffmont Rd
10.3	curve right on Caledonia Ave, then left to resume W
10.4	left on Deep Cove Rd, follow it and Dollarton Hwy back to start at 17.5 km, or **Option:** Mt Seymour Pkwy
11.4	right on Seymour Pkwy, steepish climb
12.3	Indian River Rd (to Mt Seymour) on right (Route N6)
16.0	left on Riverside Dr. (Route N5)
16.4	right on Dollarton Hwy
16.6	back at Seymour River Pl. **More information:** Deep Cove Water Taxi: 929-3011

The first major highlight of this trip is Maplewood Flats. On the heavily indus-trialized north shore of Burrard Inlet, Maplewood Flats Wildlife Sanctuary remains as a tiny vestige of the 12 km of wetland shoreline that previously existed. The diversity of habitats on this 30 ha site, including willow-hardhack swamp, mud flat, deciduous forest, and wet meadow, makes it especially valuable to wildlife. For instance, 185 species of birds have been seen here, salmon and trout feed just offshore, and in the early morning you are likely to see not only small mammals, but also deer and perhaps bear. It is thanks to the dedicated efforts of area residents, naturalists, and environmental groups that this small area survives and has finally been protected.

The old Dollar Mill: only crumbling foundations remain.

Cates Park, the next point of interest, is also on the shore. A fine local park, it features picnicking, sunbathing, and swimming. Its wooded setting provides for pleasant strolling. Make sure to see the handsome totem pole and *The Checkerboard*, a canoe carved by Chief Henry George in 1920-21. Also noteworthy are the "ancient anchor" and the many stumps with trees growing out of them. A short ride brings you to a curious circular concrete structure at the north end of the park, the furnace room foundation of the World War I Dollar Mill. The town arising around this sawmill gave the road its name. Beachview Drive does provide noble views, but of Indian Arm and of Belcarra on its far side, rather than of the near shore as you might expect.

Coming into Deep Cove, be sure to notice the bicycle shop with the stained glass sign that has taken over a former automotive service station. The rest of the downtown architecture is perhaps a little short of inspirational, but dining choices are many, from pizza and donut shops on up.

Deep Cove is well invested with parks; did you pack a picnic lunch and swimsuit? If you have made advance arrangements you might be whisked away by water taxi from the wharf beyond the foot of Gallant Avenue to continue your trip at Belcarra Bay. (If not, an interesting option to hope for in the future is the possibility of cycling on or near the shoreline east from here and around past Cove Cliff towards Dollarton. About 0.2 km of trail through Wickenden Park could make it a reality, using roads the rest of the way.) The last question is whether to return via Dollarton Highway or Mount Seymour Parkway. The latter choice admittedly does not have a great deal to offer, though it does boast bike lanes for 40% of the way.

RIGHT: Some trails are best enjoyed on foot - near Cable Pool at Capilano.

RICHMOND & DELTA

Richmond and Delta offer fun waterfront dyke rides and picturesque rural scenery, as well as swimming, insight into B.C.'s fishing industry, and nature observation. Most of these are on the flat delta lands of the Fraser River, though there are a few ascents and descents on the routes that go east towards Surrey or south to Tsawwassen.

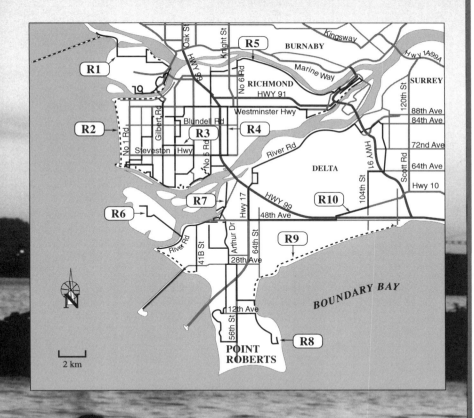

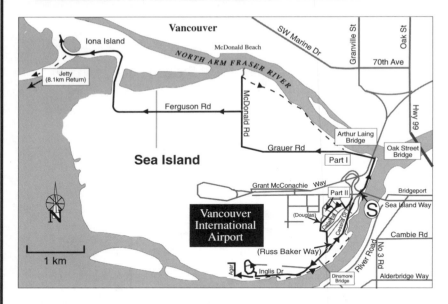

Distance and Elev Gain	(Pt I) 17.7 km, nil, return; (Pt I & II) 27.0 km, nil, return
Terrain, Road, Traffic	flat; quiet paved roads and 2.7 km of gravel and dirt road, muddy when wet (Pt II has some busier sections and a further 2.3 km of gravel road and trail)
Difficulty	F2 T2 (T3 with Part II)
Bike	something that will handle a bit of slightly rough gravel, fatter tires preferred (gravel parts are avoidable)
Access	from NW Richmond take Sea Island Way W just across the bridge to Sea Island; from Vancouver, take Arthur Laing Bridge from SW Marine Dr. (E from foot of Granville St), take first exit ("Airport Terminal South"), turn left at first light, then left again (Route R2)
Short Description	a road and dyke route along the N (and S) shores of Sea Island, with superb birding opportunities and chances to see planes, river traffic, and sewage treatment facilities, with a visit to pleasant Burkeville
Note	If the third runway is built, some directions for Part I will need modification but access to Iona Pk should be maintained.

ROAD LOG

Part I

0.0 Airport Rd at Sea Island Way

0.7 left on Grauer Rd; 2020 Airport Rd on right: North Fraser Harbour Commission, weekdays (273-1866)

1.1	dyke access on right
3.2	curve right onto McDonald Rd, past former Cora Brown subdivision
3.4	O'Grady Farm: old barn, machinery, on left at 1511
3.9	left on Ferguson Rd; many blackberry bushes
6.3	ignore "Private Road" sign
6.8	McDonald Slough on right
7.3	curve left; sewage treatment plant on right, 7 am-3 pm (261-6321)
7.5	Iona Beach Pk (GVRD: 224-5739)
8.1	jetty on left (8.1 km return)
8.4	boardwalk on right, washrooms on left
8.5	end of parking lot; **turn around** and return via same route
13.0	left on McDonald Rd
13.5	heron slough
13.6	McDonald Beach Pk, washrooms at bait shop
13.9	exit E on dyke trail near mouth of parking lot
16.6	left on Grauer Rd
	Option: to Vancouver at 17.3 bear right past a gate to get onto bridge access
17.7	back at starting point
	Part II
17.8	use crosswalks to end up at SW corner of intersection, go between chain link fence and hedge to emerge on Catalina Cr.; entering Burkeville
18.0	bear right at fork
18.2	right on Hudson Ave
18.3	left on Douglas Cr.
18.9	left on Wellington Cr.; curve left; airplane viewing, green space
19.0	right on busy Russ Baker Way/ Inglis Dr. (Route R2)
20.5	old airport buildings on right
20.7	misc. small aircraft parking on right, float planes on left
20.8	right on Cowley Cr. (one-way loop from 21.0 to 21.8) for more airplane viewing
21.5	airport S Terminal
22.0	right on Inglis Dr.
22.6	curve right on Agar Dr.
23.0	helicopter area; **turn around**
23.9	begin limestone trail at red mailbox on right **(use care)**
24.9	keep right through parking lot
25.2	Dinsmore Bridge; walk across road to continue on gravel road
26.2	right on Cessna Dr.
27.0	back at starting point

It's fun to guess where the river traffic is headed.

Sea Island has changed a lot since Hugh McRoberts began farming here in 1862. The coming of the airport to its present site in 1931, and its subsequent growth to occupy over half the island, has certainly been the biggest cause of the changes.

Of the town of Eburne, which flourished around Harry Eburne's store and post office around the turn of the century, nothing remains but a commemorative plaque outside the North Fraser Harbour Commission Office under the Arthur Laing Bridge. (This office has information on the management of the industrial, commercial, and recreational uses of the Fraser's North and Middle Arms.)

The vanished Cora Brown subdivision south of McDonald Beach is now evident only by groupings of exotic trees and occasional remnants of asphalt and concrete among the high grass and bushes. A few farms remain nearby.

Commemorative statue at the North Fraser Harbour Commission.

As you ride out to Iona Park, you'll discover that the wealth of wild and feral vegetation makes this area popular with songbirds such as swallows, goldfinches, and robins. From the Iona Island causeway you'll see shorebirds and waterfowl. McDonald Slough is also an important log storage area, as is the north shore of Iona Island.

There isn't much traffic on these roads, most of it being recreational, or, during working hours, sewage tanker trucks. Since you'll be passing by, why not stop in at the sewage treatment plant to see what happens there? (For a full 1.5 hour tour, you need to book two weeks in advance; otherwise you can still sneak a peek at the control centre and the big methane-powered turbines but the staff might not have time to explain anything.) The treated sewage used to flow directly out onto Sturgeon Bank, but as of 1988 it gets pumped 4.5 km out into Georgia Strait, 90 m below the surface. Sturgeon Bank is recovering well.

Iona Beach Park is better suited for picnicking and bird watching than for swimming. Mallards, gadwalls, three kinds of teal, ruddy ducks, shovelers, pintails, loons, grebes, great blue herons, several species of owls, other raptorial birds, and many shorebirds have all been seen here. For panoramic views, climb an observation tower or ride (or walk) out along the south jetty.

On the way back, picnic tables on the small spit at McDonald Beach let you watch the tugs cruise by while you eat. For a more rugged dining experience on the sandy river beach, go 200 m upstream. Rounding out your return via the dyke trail is a pleasant ride (although it gets a little rough and sometimes muddy) past bird-rich fields and flowering riverbank shrubs and trees.

Continuing with Part II takes you through Burkeville, with its modest houses, as relaxed a residential area (except for the jets) as you'll find anywhere. You then pass the older part of the airport with many opportunities to see a variety of planes taking off, landing, or parked, and return along the banks of the Fraser's Middle Arm.

Curious horses pause in their grazing along Ferguson Road.

R2 • *Nature Ride to Historic Steveston*

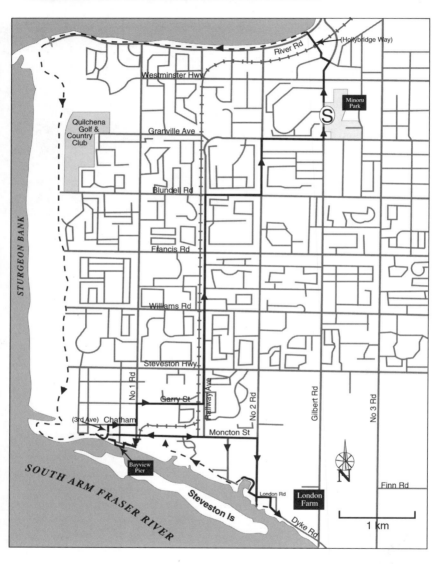

Distance and Elev Gain 27.4 km, nil, return

Terrain, Road Traffic flat; 11 km on firm gravel dyke trails, 1.6 km on paved bike lanes, 2.7 km on 4-lane arterials; worst part is the first 0.7 km

Difficulty F2 T2

Bike any bike that can handle a little gravel

Access head 0.5 km S on Gilbert Rd from Westminster Hwy in NW Richmond; option: take BC Transit to Steveston (currently route 401, 402, or 406), and rent a bike at Steveston Bicycles, picking up the route at the 20.2 km mark (Routes R1, R3, R4)

Short Description beginning at beautiful Minoru Park, the route follows great dyke trails, with many opportunities for nature viewing, and passing the Lower Mainland's best-preserved fish canneries, taking in a bike lane and Every House in Richmond on the return

---

ROAD LOG

0.0 6560 Gilbert: Richmond Family Place/Gateway Theatre/Minoru Chapel parking lot entrance; head N

0.7 left on Elmbridge Way

0.8 right on Hollybridge Way

1.2 cross River Road and head L on limestone dyke path (Route R1)

2.4 pier, for a better view

2.6 seaplane docks across river

4.4 follow shoreline to avoid parking area; viewpoint and interpretation sign; 2840 on left: Terra Nova Residence

4.9 picnic tables and toilets

5.0 interpretation sign

5.1 paved road on left ends; Sturgeon Bank ahead

6.9 small ponds beckon to be investigated

7.1 blackberry bonanza!

9.9 water lilies in ditch

Garry Point allows cyclists a close-up view of river traffic.

10.6 right just before black and yellow barrier, keeping right for best views of fish boats in Scotch Pond; Garry Point Park

11.1 short trail out to the point

11.7 bear right around Japanese garden; wander right for best view of fishing boats

12.3 on pavement; Gulf of Georgia Cannery National Historic Site; 12138 4th Ave: temporary visitor centre, free, daily in summer 10 am-5 pm (272-5045); follow along dyke/cannery fence

12.4 left on 3rd Ave

12.5 right on Moncton St; 3420B on right: Richmond Danish Bakery

12.7 3811 on left: Steveston Museum and post office, free, Mon-Sat 9:30 am-1 pm and 1:30 pm-5 pm (271-6868); 1st Ave with Moncton Market and Country Mouse to right

13.0	on left: Steveston Park, Martial Arts Centre, Japanese-Canadian Cultural Centre
14.5	right on No. 2 Rd
15.3	left on Dyke Rd, S-bend
15.7	rock wall to Shady (Steveston) Island on right
16.0	5611 on left: London Farm, donation, Sun 1-4 pm (summer Wed-Fri from 10 am) (271-5220), washrooms open 9 am-9 pm (Route R3)
16.2	Gilbert Beach; **turn around**
16.9	straight on gravel, then curve right
17.1	left on paved Dyke Rd
17.3	S-bend at Paramount Boat Basin
17.8	Paramount facility on left
17.9	road turns to gravel
18.1	on left: 1890 Britannia Cannery/Shipyard (under restoration, opening soon); take path and curve N
18.8	left on Moncton St
19.3	left on No. 1 Rd (curves onto Bayview St)
19.6	left onto Bayview Pier; walk bike along dock
19.8	right on 3rd Ave
20.0	right on Chatham St
20.2	3731 on left: Steveston Bicycles in old church, rentals/repairs (271-5544)
20.4	left on No. 1 Rd
20.7	right on Garry St
21.6	left on Railway Ave
23.7	bike lane from Francis Rd
24.5	right on Blundell Rd (note: bike lane eradicated for convenience of car drivers)
25.3	left on No. 2 Rd
25.5	7620 on right: Every House
26.1	rejoin bike route at Granville Ave
26.9	left on Gilbert Rd
27.4	back at Minoru Pk
	More information: Richmond Museum: 276-4012
	Special Projects (Britannia Shipyard, Scotch Pond): 276-4107

Minoru Park, with its sports and arts facilities and new (1992) museum, hides at its heart a picturesque arrangement of ponds and gardens and an architectural gem, the (relocated) 1891 Minoru Chapel.

On reaching the dyke, you are treated to car-free cycling with splendid views of the airport and the North Shore mountains. As you near the ocean, imagine what it must have been like before the dykes, when this area was seasonally flooded, scrubby meadow and the Coast Salish camped here to catch eulachons, sturgeon, and salmon. (This area was to become known for its canneries from 1892 until 1928.) Farming was begun by five Newfoundlanders around 1890. Only a tiny piece of the Terra Nova farmlands has been spared from housing developments. The best intact farmstead is the Terra Nova Residence.

Rounding the bend, you come to the fertile estuary of Sturgeon Bank. Shifting sediments and seasonal variations in temperature and salinity restrict the number of species that can live here, but those that can, do so in abundance. Immature fish and crustaceans thrive in the shallow, muddy, nutrient-rich waters. Secure from many water predators, they nevertheless become meals for shorebirds, migrating ducks and geese, and hungry herons.

Along the dyke, the elderberry, broom, blackberry, birch, and small plants are land-lords and caterers to a variety of songbirds. As the vistas open up once again, you are treated to panoramic views of the Lions, Pt Grey, Bowen Island, the Sunshine Coast, the Gulf Islands . . . and cattle grazing peacefully. Out past the cattails, sedges, and rushes, the low tide bares sand and mud flats, promising to lead you to distant shores, but don't be misled; they only go out 6 or 7 km. At the end of the dyke trail is Garry Point Park. Tarry here at the narrow mouth of the shipping channel to enjoy one of the absolutely best viewpoints for observing the marine traffic plying the Fraser's busy South Arm.

Shopfront murals in Steveston.

Steveston, a fish processing centre from the 1890s, retains more of this heritage than anywhere else in the Lower Mainland. The 1894 Gulf of Georgia Cannery, the westernmost one remaining, was at one time the second largest salmon cannery in BC. It is now a national historic site scheduled to be fully open to the public in 1994. Meanwhile, the visitors' centre is to the left on 4th Ave (Ask here for area guides.)

On Moncton Street be sure to visit the Richmond Danish Bakery to sample a superb selection of pastries, especially the danishes! Energies replenished, you'll find Moncton Street also to be home to antique shops, purveyors of fishing gear and marine hardware, and fish-and-chips restaurants, should you still be hungry. Steveston Museum, built in 1906 as a bank, doubles as a post office. On the main floor, be sure to see the Dictaphone in the recreated period office. At 1st Ave, Moncton Market offers wholesome produce, while Country Mouse, just to the south, is about the best place around for ceramic and other crafts.

Leaving the new residential developments behind, you encounter more rural surroundings. Shady (Steveston) Island is a superb study in natural succession, with 100 species of plants inhabiting a variety of niches. Over 60 species of birds use the island or its immediate area. The rock wall leading to Shady Island has deteriorated, so it's rough going and you're sure to get wet; watch the tides or you may be spending the night! Nearby are the historic London Farmhouse and Gilbert Beach.

Ponds dot the salt marsh along Sturgeon Bank.

Returning along the shore to town, your route passes colourful modern fishing marinas and historic sites (open soon), and includes a visit to the redeveloped Bayview Pier area. Then, on the way out of Steveston, notice Steveston Bicycles in its former church, ride part of Richmond's well-marked official bike route, and pass the 1911 former residence of Captain John Every. Now you can boast to your friends that you've seen Every House in Richmond!

RIGHT: Even new bikes need regular safety checks.

R3 • *South Richmond Strawberry Gathering Expedition*

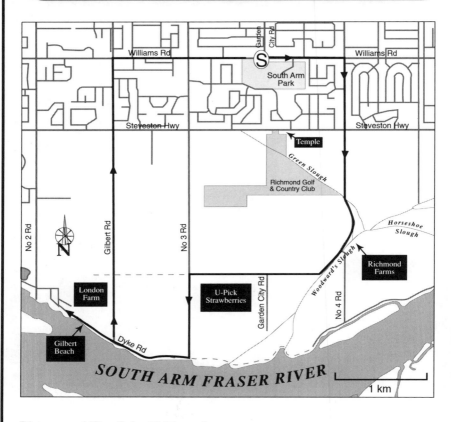

Distance and Elev Gain	12.0 km, nil, return
Terrain, Road, Traffic	flat; paved roads; 7 km on low-traffic rural roads with the rest on residential arterials with low-to-moderate traffic
Difficulty	F1 T2
Bike	any bike
Access	take Garden City Rd to its junction with Williams Rd 5.5 km S of Sea Island Way (careful not to curve onto Granville Ave); or join the route at No. 4 Rd, 2 km W of Hwy 99 cloverleaf along Steveston Hwy (Routes R2, R4)
Short Description	a short journey to the farmlands of S Richmond to gather some mouthwatering strawberries, followed by a visit to a bird watching beach and picnic area

ROAD LOG

0.0 Williams Rd at Garden City Rd, entrance to South Arm Community Pk at community hall; head E

0.2 South Arm Pool on right

0.8 right on No. 4 Rd

1.6 cross Steveston Hwy (0.7 km to right at 9160 Steveston Hwy: the International Buddhist Society Temple, free, 10 am-5 pm, groups must book ahead (274-2822))

2.2 11620 on left: handsome cream coloured heritage home with dual brick chimneys is the 1912 *Goldie Harris House*, later the residence of Reeve Thomas Kidd; barn is c. 1913

3.0 U-pick strawberry fields at Richmond Farms on the left just SE of where No. 4 Rd meets Finn Road; continue W on Finn Rd

3.2 9711 on right: handsome *Eldstrom House*, built c. 1912 by Finnish settlers.

3.7 U-pick strawberries on left

3.9 pass Garden City Rd on left

4.7 left on No. 3 Rd (Route R4)

5.6 right on Dyke Rd

6.4 pass Gilbert Rd

6.6 Gilbert Beach begins on left (Route R2)

6.8 6511 on right: London Farm, donation, Sun 1-4 pm (summer Wed-Fri from 10 am) (271-5220), washrooms open 9 am-9 pm; **turn around**

7.2 left on Gilbert Rd

8.5 cross Steveston Hwy

10.3 right on Williams Rd

11.1 cross No. 3 Rd

11.6 South Arm Pk appears

12.0 back at Garden City Rd

Dyke Rd offers pleasant cycling.

Sure, you can go to the supermarket and buy berries imported from California, but there's nothing quite like the satisfying taste of luscious, vine-fresh strawberries that you've just picked yourself. So, even though this ride gives you two U-pick places to choose from, it's a good idea to get there by mid-morning, lest they sell out before you arrive, leaving your mouth watering with nothing to put into it. Early summer is, of course, the best time to go in search of strawberries, but this is still a pleasant, shorter ride throughout the rest of the year.

Once you cross Steveston Highway, the rural/urban boundary, it's as if you're in a different world. Pastures and corn fields line both sides of the road. Here and there, the fields are ornamented by stately heritage homes, venerable barns, and settler-planted trees. The air is populated by those aerial acrobats, the swallows, performing incredible rolls and swoops in pursuit of insects. Ducks, and often herons, make use of the wide drainage ditches and sloughs.

Before white settlers came and built roads, the native Indians travelled by canoe through the sloughs that served as their transportation network.

Youngsters enjoy meeting the barnyard fowl at London farm.

Once you have your strawberries safely in hand (or in backpack), head south to the banks of the Fraser to enjoy them either on the shore at Gilbert Beach, or across the road in the picnic area at London Farm. London Farmhouse was built in 1898 by Charles London, who settled here in 1875. Open to the public, its period rooms bring back bygone days. Gilbert Beach is a sandy stretch of riverbank where you can relax against a log and watch for feathered friends, including hawks, owls, cormorants, grebes, and other varieties, and for seals. Eventually, it's time to head back through farmland to the suburbs, hopefully with a few tasty strawberries packed away for later.

As an option, especially if it's not strawberry season, you might want to take a detour along (admittedly busy) Steveston Highway to see a splendid Buddhist temple. A visit to the structure, described as the most exquisite example of Chinese palatial architecture in North America, is a mini-excursion into traditional Chinese culture.

RIGHT: Mmmmm . . . the incomparable flavour of fresh strawberries.

R4 • *Richmond Nature Park and Finn Slough*

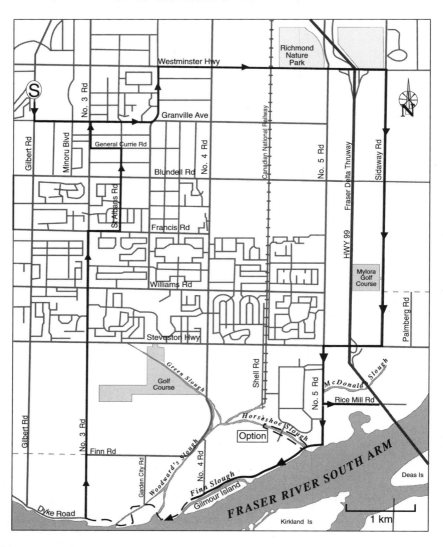

Distance and Elev Gain	25.9 km, nil, return
Terrain, Road, Traffic	flat; 1.5 km on gravel dyke track, otherwise mostly on quiet roads, with 10.8 km along busier roads, of which 2.2 km have bike lanes and 3.4 km have paved shoulders
Difficulty	F2 T3
Bike	any bike that can handle a little gravel

Access head 0.5 km S on Gilbert Rd from Westminster Hwy in
NW Richmond (Routes R2, R3, R5)

Short Description from beautiful Minoru Pk to Richmond Nature Pk,
through farmland and along the Fraser to picturesque Finn
Slough, and back past an attractive 1919 schoolhouse

ROAD LOG

0.0 6560 Gilbert Road: Richmond Family Place/Gateway Theatre Minoru Chapel
parking lot entrance (Richmond Museum nearby); head S

0.4 left on Granville Ave bike lane

1.7 end of bike lane at St Albans Rd

2.0 curve left to join Garden City Way (you can avoid merging traffic by
using crosswalk to E)

2.9 right on Westminster Hwy

4.9 11300 on right: geodesic dome house

5.2 Richmond Nature Pk on left, free, 273-7015

5.8 Caution: *traffic merging and crossing at Hwy 99*

6.3 Richmond Nature Study Centre on left

6.3 right on Sidaway Rd

8.8 9360 on left: birch wood and decorative Lowland Stables

9.6 golf course entrance; optional dirt road opposite and slightly S

10.4 right on Steveston Hwy

10.6 on left: Bavarian ranch-style castle of the strawberry king or a produce stand?

10.6 Caution: *merging traffic at Hwy 99*

11.1 Fantasy Gardens on right

11.2 left on No. 5 Rd

12.0 left on Rice Mill Rd

12.7 Richmond Model Flying Site, seasonal bike
tunnel-shuttle pickup, BC Ferries
repair docks; **return**

13.4 left on No. 5 Rd

14.0 right on Dyke Rd

14.2 Horseshoe Slough (across from pumping
station)
Option: 1.4 km unpaved loop to "bridge of
rusty reflections"

15.6 foot of No. 4 Rd; Finn Slough; wooden bridge
to Gilmour Is., boards removable to let small
boats pass

16.0 continue on gravel dyke track

16.5 go around paper mill

17.4 rejoin dyke

*On the high tide these boats
will float once more.*

18.0	right on No. 3 Rd (Route R3)
22.2	right on Francis Rd
22.6	left on St Albans Rd
23.9	left on Gen. Currie Rd
24.1	8200 on left: General Currie School
24.3	right on No. 3 Rd
24.6	left on Granville Ave bicycle lane
25.5	right on Gilbert Rd
25.9	back at start

More information: Richmond Museum: 276-4012

Minoru Park has a lot to offer, but so does another Richmond park. If you've got anything of a naturalist spirit, you're bound to enjoy 87 ha Richmond Nature Park. The boardwalks and walking trails of the western half lead through bog and pond habitat now scarce in Richmond. At its edge is a lookout platform giving an eagle-eye view of the waterfowl below. However, the clinching reason for stopping here is the nature house. Yes, there are interpretation guides, and a library, but it's the many hands-on displays — the ones that let you peer through a microscope at the universe within a drop of pond water, stamp the footprint of a rabbit, or watch bees making honey so close by that you can feel their warmth — that make it a hit with young and old. The eastern half of the park (Richmond Nature Study Centre), across Hwy 99, has as yet only a walking trail.

The observation platform gives a commanding view of the pond at Richmond Nature Park.

Fortunately, you have the services of an official bike route and paved shoulders to help you travel most of the way from one park to the other. You then continue through farmland, passing pine woods, fields of potatoes, blueberries, and cranberries, and more than a few houses that suggest that the days when the farm children sleep three to a bed are drawing to an end in this part of Richmond. (If you have a mountain bike, you may be tempted to explore the sometimes bumpy, between-the-fields road across from the Mylora Golf Course. It leads east to Triangle Road. Take it east to the dyke, then turn right onto the dyke to arrive at Fraser Wharves at the end of Steveston Hwy.)

After escaping a fragrant industrial area, you might be mislead by the sight of ferries to think you're in Tsawwassen, but this is the BC Ferry Corporation's refit facility.

(Nearby is the tunnel shuttle pickup point if you really do want to catch a ferry.) Westbound along the shore of the Fraser, with its views of the low, wooded islands clustering against the Ladner shoreline, it's fun to detour inland along Horseshoe Slough to the "bridge of rusty reflections," returning past great quantities of blackberry bushes.

Between shrubby, undeveloped Gilmour Island and Dyke Road is Finn Slough; on its banks is a colourful fishing community on stilts, its Finnish roots in the 1890s. If you venture onto the rickety wooden bridge that leads to the island, you may meet the very affectionate cat that lives nearby.

After circumnavigating a paper mill, you pass a grassy section of dyke that might be just the spot for a picnic, then it's back towards the city through farm land. Nestled amongst the lavish new townhouses and apartments south of Granville is a notable holdout: the red and white General Currie School, with a beautiful, heavily-timbered front porch. After over 70 years, it's still in service.

Minoru Park is excellent for a stroll before or after a bike ride.

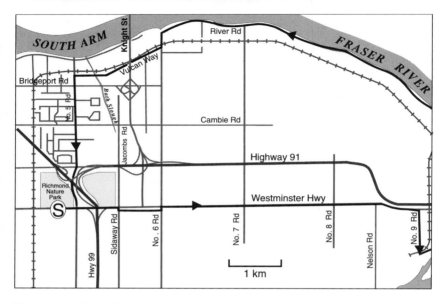

Distance and Elev Gain 30.4 km, nil, return

Terrain, Road, Traffic flat; about 4.5 km of gravel, busier section along Westminster Hwy has narrow paved shoulder; mostly quiet

Difficulty F2 T3

Bike any bike that can handle a little gravel

Access take Westminster Hwy 1.4 km E from No 5 Rd or 0.6 km W of Hwy 99 (Route R4)

Short Description a trip through the farmlands of eastern Richmond and along the Fraser River, passing strawberry U-pick farms, an ornate Sikh temple, an enormous 12-sided barn, an especially interesting marina, and some residual bog forest

---

ROAD LOG

0.0 Westminster Hwy at Richmond Nature Pk; head E

0.6 Caution: *merging and crossing traffic at overpass*

1.1 Richmond Nature Study Centre on left; turn right, then left onto lesser-used roadway

2.0 rejoin active section of Westminster Hwy at No. 6 Rd

3.6 No. 7 Rd; 0.5 km left for U-pick strawberries

5.3 No. 8 Rd; about 0.8 km right for U-pick strawberries

5.8 18691 on left: Nanaksar Gursikh Temple

7.0 right on No. 9 Rd

7.8 7071 on right: Ewen Round Barn

7.9 left, then right on paved road

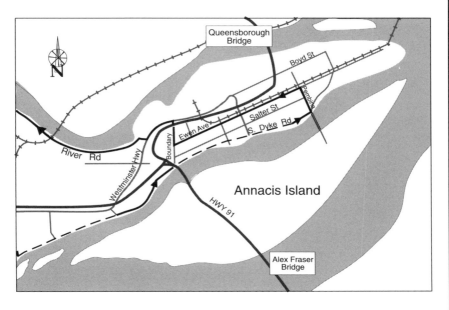

- **8.2** left on gravel dyke
- **8.7** on pavement
- **9.0** Shelter Island Marina and boat yard; access to Graybar Rd
- **9.3** on gravel
- **10.1** on pavement; access to Westminster Hwy
- **11.3** heavy duty fishboats
- **11.4** majestic weeping willows on right
- **11.9** pass under Hwy 91 Annacis Island bridge, continue on gravel on S Dyke Rd
- **14.1** left on Pembina St at bridge to Annacis Is.
- **14.2** one-engine fire hall on right
- **14.5** left on Ewen Ave
- **16.3** right on Boundary Rd
- **16.4** under Hwy 91
- **16.5** left on Westminster Hwy
- **17.1** right on River Rd (don't miss it!) and then curve left along river
- **19.0** swing-span railway bridge, 1920; East Richmond Woodland on left
- **19.5** cranberry fields on left
- **21.3** country lane feeling with buildings right next to road

Blue and white tiles distinguish exotic-looking Nanaksar Gursikh Temple.

24.0	bridges to fire hydrants
25.7	curve left
26.0	right on Vulcan Way; **Caution: *diagonal track crossings***
27.7	left on No. 5 Rd
28.8	small park on left side
29.5	beginning of overpasses
30.3	right on Westminster Hwy
30.4	Richmond Nature Pk

If you have the good fortune for it to be early summer as you head east from Richmond Nature Park, in addition to the farms and tree nurseries you'll encounter tempting signs announcing fresh raspberries and strawberries. After an appropriate break, a few more minutes of pedalling bring you to the Nanaksar Gursikh Temple, tiled in glistening blue, orange, and white.

Now heading south on a quiet country road, you are faced with the contrast between the great circa 1893 Ewen cattle barn and the Lafarge cement plant that rises just behind it. This twelve-sided barn, representing the state-of-the-art for its time, is believed to be the only one of its kind west of Quebec. Built to hold 900 tonnes of hay while feeding 100 cows, this 96 m diameter structure survives as Richmond's premier agricultural heritage building.

Reaching the dyke, you proceed for the next while mostly on hard-packed gravel as you follow the Fraser upriver. Just offshore are the luxuriantly wooded Lion and Don Islands. Nearby is the Shelter Island Marina, certainly one of the most colourful marinas on the Lower Mainland. Here you will find an engaging mix of modern yachts, fine older ships, and marvelously creative live-aboards. Two kilometres further, sturdy aluminum fishboats line the shore, and beyond stand a hodgepodge of fishing-related small industries and commercial fishers' homes.

The eastern end of Lulu Island, Queensborough, retains the name originally proposed by Governor James Douglas for the entire city of New Westminster. It forms part of the city's industrialized zone and adjacent residential area. The 1911 rail bridge at the very tip, which replaced an 1891 road bridge, was shared with cars until a new four-lane bridge was built further west in 1960. When Highway 91A opened in 1986, local businesses along the main street were bypassed. The return leg begins by following the North Arm of the Fraser River. Along the more easterly sections, riverbank access is unobstructed; later it is interrupted by occasional houses and industry. Morning often reveals herons standing sentry on the river's edge, each on its own piling. Riverside cottonwoods and the birch, pine, and alder of East Richmond Woodland provide welcome greenery. Industry becomes more prevalent and is then replaced by commercial and rural-residential realms as you approach the end of the ride.

RIGHT: Shelter Island Marina: one of the Lower Mainland's most colourful.

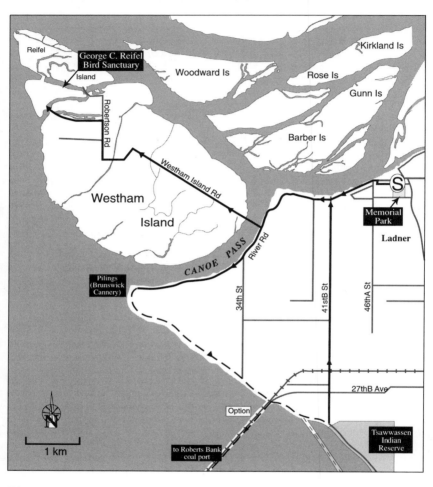

Distance and Elev Gain	27.3 km, nil, return
Terrain, Road, Traffic	flat; paved with about 5.3 km of fair-to-good gravel dyke trail; otherwise low-to-moderate use roads
Difficulty	F2 T3
Bike	any bike except fine racers; knobby tires are handy
Access	take Hwy 17 S from Hwy 99 and turn right on 48th Ave (at Hwy 10); it becomes 47A Ave in downtown Ladner; take Delta St (second left past Elliot) 1 block S (Routes R7, R8)

Short Description a ride through farming country to a bird sanctuary, and along a pretty seaside dyke trail, with the option to ride out to the Roberts Bank coal terminal

ROAD LOG

0.0	N side of Memorial Pk, on 47th Ave/Victoria at Delta St; head W
0.5	right on 47A St
0.6	left on 47A Ave/Stanley, becomes River Rd
2.0	pass 41B St/C.B. Main Rd; blackberries on dyke top; 0.3 km dyke trail
3.7	right on Westham Is. Rd bridge, slightly hidden; **Caution: *mismatched board edges and slippery when wet***
5.2	Lea Black Currants/Raspberries on right
5.9	2630 on left: Pan's Garden, call for hours (946-0583)
6.9	2170 on left: Bisset's Berry Farm U-pick berries, many kinds
7.1	curve onto Robertson Rd
7.9	left to Reifel Sanctuary (straight ahead at 5421 Robertson Rd: Alaksen Wildlife Area/Cdn Wildlife Service Pac. and Yukon Reg. Office at 5421 Robertson Rd; open 8:30-4:30, closed weekends and stat. holidays)
8.9	Reifel Bird Sanctuary (946-6980), $3.25, daily 9 am-4 pm, washrooms; **return via same route**
14.0	right on River Rd
16.0	dyke becomes accessible at "no hunting or trespassing" sign, gravel track on top
16.5	gate; climb dyke here, or keep right on gravel road beyond to reach dyke at 16.8
16.7	pilings are remains of Brunswick Cannery
20.3	straight through gate; and cross tracks and 27B Ave/Matheson Rd **Option**: 9.2 km round trip along causeway to Roberts Bank coal port; **Caution: *diagonal railway crossings***
20.9	bear left at fork
21.2	left on 41B St at Tsawwassen Rd
25.3	right on River Rd
26.7	right on 47A St
26.8	left on 47th Ave
27.3	back at Delta St

Heading out of town, you pass farms and fishing-related industries. Just past 41B St you can ride the high, grassy dyke for a while, and there are blackberries. Crossing the swing bridge to Westham Island, watch for herons in Canoe Passage. The dykes that encircle the island would undoubtedly make for some fine cycling if arrangements could be made with the owners to open them to the public.

Westham Island is largely devoted to farming; you will find fields of potatoes, corn, cabbage, and grass. There are also at least two berry outlets. If you're an organic home gardener, spring is a good time to stop in at Pan's Garden, a small but thorough supplier of seeds, bedding plants, tools, compost, advice, and other needs for healthy produce.

Listen for the faint echoes of the bustling cannery that once stood here.

The far end of Westham Island is devoted to wildlife habitat. The Alaksen National Wildlife Area comprises 648 ha of Ramsar wetlands of international significance, enhanced through the creation of artificial seasonally flooded meadows. Adjacent is the Reifel Bird Sanctuary. It serves as a vital wintering area and migratory stopover from October to March, with waterfowl nesting and raising of young continuing until June. Although there aren't as many birds in the summer, it's still worth a visit. Over 230 species have been seen here, including mallard, pintail, snow goose, Canada goose, teal, wood duck, redhead, hawks, bald eagles, owls, marsh wrens, and blackbirds. Before these two refuges were established, hungry waterfowl would stay way out at sea until nightfall, after which they knew they could come in and feed in the fields in relative safety from hunters.

As you continue southwest, the eerie silhouette of the Roberts Bank coal port looms on the skyline. Nearing Brunswick Point, you note a wild openness not found along Richmond's dykes. At the point itself, you will see only the pilings remaining from the cannery that once stood here, the many flowers growing among them forming living bouquets in bright purples, yellows, and white. This area, like the Reifel Sanctuary, makes for some great bird viewing. At low tide, the exposed sand and mud flats reach out several kilometres beyond the brackish marsh with its sedges, rushes, cattails, loosestrife, and arrowhead. Further along, you'll also see strange little grassy hummocks rising from the sand.

If the road isn't too busy, on a Sunday maybe, why not ride out to the coal port? You might think coal is coal, but did you know that they ship 127 grades of it from here? Most is for steelmaking, but some is for nuclear applications; it's so pure that it smoulders in contact with the air! You won't get to see anything up close, but if it's a slow day, perhaps the commissary who guards the end of the road will be in the mood to chat.

There's one more kilometre to cycle along the dyke before you reach the Tsawwassen Indian Reserve, then you head back towards town.

RIGHT: If you need a bike for the day, why not rent one?

R7 • *Ladner Waterfront*

Distance and Elev Gain	7.8 km, nil, return
Terrain, Road, Traffic	flat; good roads with option for some gravel; mostly quiet roads, but busier along River Rd and Elliot St, especially at rush hour
Difficulty	F1 T2
Bike	any bike
Access	take Hwy 17 S from Hwy 99 and turn right on 48th Ave (at Hwy 10) — it becomes 47 A Ave in downtown Ladner — and encounter route at Delta St (second street past Elliot) (Routes R6, R8)
Short Description	a short ride along the Ladner-area river front, with lots of opportunities for bird watching, and a visit to a local museum

ROAD LOG

0.0 N side of Memorial Pk, on 47th Ave at Delta St; head N

0.1 old church on right houses Montessori School

0.2 cross 48th Ave; on right: solid brick post office

0.3 4858 on right: Delta Museum, Tue-Sat 10 am-3:30 pm, Sun 2-4 pm (archives Tue-Sat 10 am-3 pm) (946-9322)

0.5 right on Chisholm St

0.6 curve right onto Elliot St

0.7 left on River Rd

1.0 5011 on left: Ladner Yacht Club

1.1 pass Ladner Harbour Pk turnoff

1.5 left on Ferry Rd

2.8 series of lagoons on left for draining water from the residential property across the street

3.1 end of the road; decaying ferry dock; **Caution: *rotted through in places; Captain's Cove Marina and Restaurant/Pub on right;* head back**

4.7 right on River Rd

5.0 right over bridge

5.4 right to Ladner Harbour Pk (straight for fish boat docks)

5.6 Ladner Harbour Pk, dawn to dusk, picnic facilities, water, washrooms; **return same way**

Option: to tip of island (c. 2 km return)

Take Swenson Walk, a broad trail headed SW from the picnic area loop, to join a paved/gravel road passing the fishboat harbour. Continue around a large sandy loop at the point, returning down the road, passing where you first turned in to the park.

6.2 right on River Rd

6.7 right on Elliot St to curve around onto Chisholm St and then Georgia St

7.3 right on 48th Ave, then left on 48B St

7.6 left on 47th Ave

7.8 back at start

The Fraser River gold rush had been kind to former Californians William and Thomas Ladner. When they were looking for a place to settle, they recalled the delta lands they had seen near the mouth of the Fraser, and in 1868 became the first settlers at what was to become known as Ladners' Landing, and later simply as Ladner. During the 1870s, Ladner was a frequent paddlewheeler stop between Victoria and New Westminster, and the site of farms, fish canneries, and lumber mills.

Though there are a few handsome buildings that have survived Ladner's earlier days, head to the Delta Museum for the most thorough immersion in the town's history. On the main floor of this fine tudor style building you'll find a period nursery, bedroom, ladies' tailor, etc. The most stimulating displays are in the basement, however, where a simulated downtown street scene comes alive with the sounds as well as the sights of a bygone era.

Observe skilled artisans practicing their trades at Captain's Cove Marina.

Before the tunnel was built, a ferry carried people across the river to Woodward's Landing in Richmond. Service began in 1913, when the ferry docked close to town. In 1933 the landing point was changed to the end of Ferry Road, where it remained until the residents finally got their wish for a fixed connection in 1959. At Captain's Cove Marina you can get a closeup look at small craft pulled ashore for repairs and refits. And although you can see Deas Island just over a stone's throw away, it's a case of "you can't get there from here" — perhaps one day there will be a pedestrian/cycle route from Ladner that goes along the waterfront, bypassing Highway 17.

In the quest for residential land, the eastern side of the road has been drained and filled, but the western side remains as marshy wildlife habitat. Across from one development, pools have been created that are supposed to enhance fish and bird potential.

In the late 19th century, migrating waterfowl had a deadly surprise awaiting them at Ladner. In addition to the market hunters, who would sell their catches in New Westminster or Vancouver, everyone else seemed to be gunning for them too.

Ladner Harbour Park makes a good shady picnic stop. The road along the north shore of the harbour itself takes you past fishing boats and gear repair areas. If you're a bird watcher, you'll perhaps be more interested in keeping a watch over the adjacent former sewage lagoon and the shoreline to the west of the park. Some of the birds regularly seen in the area are red-necked phalaropes, Franklin's gulls, numerous dabbling and diving ducks, Canada geese, marsh wrens, ring-necked pheasants, ruffed grouse, marsh hawks, red-tailed hawks, bald eagles, snowy owls, and many songbirds.

RIGHT: Universal Buddhist Temple on E 49th Ave in Vancouver: dragons have more positive connotations for Asians than for Europeans.

R8 • *Tsawwassen*

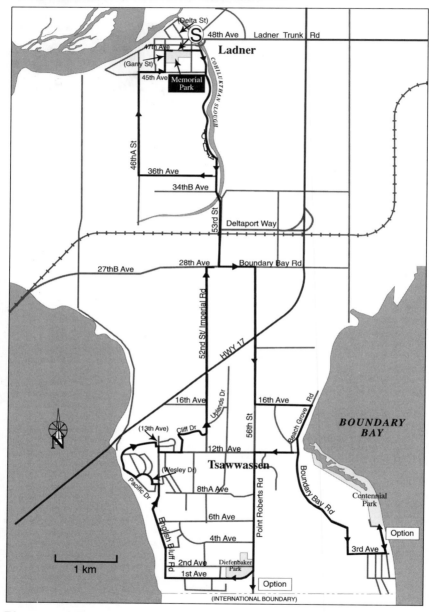

Distance and Elev Gain 34.1 km, 100 m, return

Terrain, Road, Traffic mostly flat with one gradual climb and a steep descent; paved rural and residential roads with low to moderate traffic, 3.5 km along busier 56th St, over 5 km with paved shoulders

Difficulty F3 T4

Bike good brakes needed

Access take Hwy 17 S from Hwy 99 and turn right on 48th Ave (at Hwy 10); it becomes 47 A Ave in downtown Ladner; take Delta St (second left past Elliot) 1 block S (Routes R6, R7, R9)

Short Description a trip to Centennial Beach, for swimming or bird watching, and a loop around the Tsawwassen highlands

ROAD LOG

0.0 N side of Memorial Pk, on 47th Ave at Delta St; head E

0.4 right on Arthur Dr.

1.6 Cohilukthan Slough on left

2.0 3900 on left: Augustinian Monastery

4.3 left on 28th Ave/Boundary Bay Rd

4.9 right on 56th St/Pt Roberts Rd

6.1 cross Hwy 17

7.0 S Delta Rec. Ctre on left

7.3 left on 16th Ave/Herd Rd (Route R9)

8.3 right on Beach Grove Rd; shore trail access

9.2 straight on Boundary Bay Rd at 12th Ave

11.4 curve left on 3rd Ave/Gunn St; 301 on right: old farmhouse with wraparound porch

12.1 left on Centennial Pkwy

12.6 Centennial Beach Pk, concession, change/ washrooms; **return via same route**
Option: find your way along the shoreline back to 12th Ave

15.9 left on 12th Ave

16.7 left on 56th St

19.0 right on 1st Ave/Summer Rd; Diefenbaker Pk (a former gravel pit) has pond, fountain, play area, grassy slopes, picnic tables
Option: continue on 56th St for Pt Roberts, US

20.5 right on 48th St/English Bluff Rd; occasional glimpses across the water to ferry terminal and beyond

21.2 left on Wesley Dr., past small totem pole

22.4 tiny Village Pk on left

22.7 right on Pacific Dr.

23.9 left on 12 A Ave, then right on 48th St (left on 48th leads to blackberries and a vantage point on steep hillside at corner of 13th Ave)

24.0 left on 12th Ave/Raitt Rd

24.4 left on Cliff Dr.

Friendly horses along the way always welcome a visit.

25.2	left on 52nd St/Imperial Rd
25.3	pass Uplands Dr., take in the view before you descend steep hill
26.3	cross Hwy 17
28.0	2757 on left: Deltaport Farmers' Market
28.1	right on 28th Ave
28.3	left on 53rd St, becomes Arthur Dr.
29.9	left on 36th Ave/Nelson Rd
31.3	right on 46A St/Fairview Rd
33.1	right on 45th Ave/King Edward Rd
33.7	left on Garry St
34.0	right on 47th Ave
34.1	end

Centennial Beach is a year-round beach: for swimming, volleyball, and sunbathing in the summer and for bird watching the rest of the year. Spring and fall migrations are the best times to see diving and dabbling ducks; black brant are most numerous in spring. Gulls, terns, Eurasian wigeon, and herons also make use of the mud flats while short-eared owls, great-horned owls, red-tailed hawks, harriers, rough-legged hawks, and sharp-shinned hawks keep watchful eyes on nearby fields.

On the way to Centennial Beach, you pass fertile farmlands and skirt downtown Tsawwassen. Then it's past the cottages of Beach Grove and the Spetifore farmlands, object of recent controversy between the would-be developer and environmentalists.

Once you're done at the beach, you backtrack for 3 km. Although it used to be possible to enter the US just south of here and loop through Point Roberts, these seasonal customs offices were shut down in 1975 to cut costs, leaving only the ones on 56th Street. Alternatively, you could follow the shoreline north to 12th Avenue, but only the last part is on a good trail.

Continuing on through the commercial core of Tsawwassen, you climb up a hill that thousands of years ago stood alone as an island beyond the wide mouth of the Fraser River. Today it is a quiet residential area that makes an interesting study in the differences between higher and lower priced housing over the last few decades.

Descending a steep incline — pause for the view — brings you back to the flatlands. On the return route, crops such as cabbages and pumpkins are prevalent late in the year, but you will also see old orchards, cattle, and horses.

RIGHT: Centennial Beach, Delta.

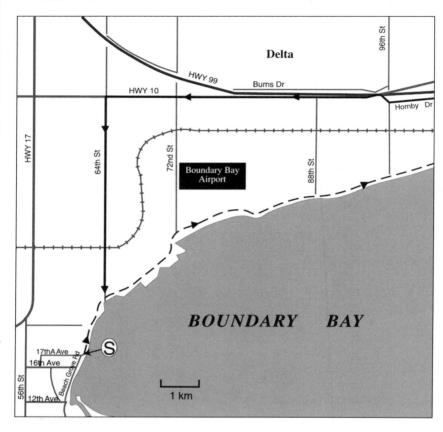

Distance and Elev Gain	12.8 km, nil, one way
Terrain, Road, Traffic	good quality gravel dyke track (option to continue on rougher track or return on road); occasional traffic on small sections of dyke
Difficulty	F2 T1
Bike	any bike except delicate racers
Access	from Hwy 17 in Delta, take 56th St/Pt Roberts Rd towards Tsawwassen, then head 1 km E on 16th Ave and 0.3 km N on Beach Grove Rd (Route R8)
Short Description	a rural waterfront ride, away from traffic, with great views and some of the Fraser Valley's finest opportunities for bird watching

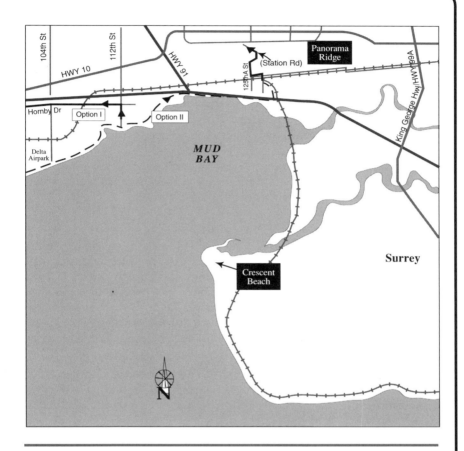

ROAD LOG

0.0 Beach Grove Rd at 17A Ave; head E on gravel path, turning left at dyke

1.9 access to 64th St/Goudy Rd; trail to water

4.2 access to 72nd St/Benson Rd

7.5 access to 88th St/Smith Rd

8.4 gate (occasional cars 'til next gate)

9.2 access to 96th St/Matthews Rd

9.9 relic pilings

10.7 Delta Airpark on left

10.9 access to 104th St/Embree Rd

12.7 pumping station at end of slough

12.8 decaying buildings; 112th St/Oliver Rd

        Option I: return to Tsawwassen; use same route or take 112th St N and turn left on Hornby Dr., continuing W on Hwy 10 and heading S on 64th St or Hwy 17 (Route R10)

Option II: continue to Surrey's Panorama Ridge; rougher track beyond gate leads parallel to Hwy 99 through scrubby, intermittent woodland; curve left at railway tracks, right on a gravel road, left on Colebrook Rd, then right up the hill on Station Rd towards Hwy 10

A few thousand years after the last great ice sheets melted 11 000 years ago, sediments deposited by the mighty Fraser began to block off its access to Boundary Bay, changing Tsawwassen/Point Roberts from an island into a peninsula as the river's channel was extended further out to sea. The land area thus created remained subject to periodic flooding until 19th century settlers constructed dykes to protect their farmland. Dyking radically affected the vegetation in the delta, destroying almost all of the floodplain forest and wet meadows; in addition, over 80% of the Boundary Bay salt marsh was destroyed. Proposals for residential and golf course developments in turn continued to put pressure on the farmland through the early 1990s.

The extensive sand and mud flats left at the former river mouth, augmented by the Serpentine and Nicomekl Rivers at the eastern end of the bay, are a productive habitat for herring spawn, crabs, ghost shrimp, and other invertebrates. These tiny creatures and the great beds of eelgrass provide food for vast numbers of fish, ocean mammals, and birds. Boundary Bay was also the single most productive oyster bed in BC until 1960, when it was closed due to contamination by sewage outfall and agricultural runoff. Although municipal sewage is now piped to treatment plants, farming residues are still a problem.

Boundary Bay is probably the best place in the Vancouver area to observe shorebirds. They tend to be most plentiful during migration, although some overwinter, and are best seen when a rising tide forces them close to shore. Species seen include various kinds of gulls, plovers, sandpipers, and godwits. Among the predator species feeding here are merlins, peregrine falcons, snowy owls, and occasionally gyrfalcons. Diving and dabbling ducks, too, overwinter here by the thousands, with great flocks of black brant arriving during migration. In all, perhaps 1.4 million birds spend part of their year here.

As you ride along the dyke, watch for the many types of wildflowers, including yarrow, goldenrod, wild roses, and gumweed. Impressive views of the San Juan Islands, the Olympic Peninsula, Mount Baker, and across the flatlands to Burnaby and the North Shore make this a fine route any time of the year. Adding historical colour, several dilapidated buildings—the remains of an oyster processing plant—perch precariously on their pilings at the foot of 112th St.

When you reach the end, you can return the same way, or take the road back. Although the directions given here take you along nearly the whole dyke, five intermediate road-access points give you the option to easily shorten the trip as you see fit. Conversely, you could ride further along the dyke, at least as far as the railway tracks, and then head up into Surrey's Panorama Ridge area.

RIGHT: What's left?

MOTOR VEHICLES
(EXCEPT IN PARKING AREAS)
HORSEBACK RIDING
GAS MODEL AIRPLANES
GOLFING • GO-CARTS
ARCHERY
PROHIBITED
IN
PUBLIC PARKS
AND
SCHOOL GROUNDS
MAXIMUM FINE $ 200
MUNICIPAL BY-LAW 1988

DOGS MUST BE ON LEASH AND UNDER CONTROL AT ALL TIMES. IT IS AN OFFENCE TO LEAVE DOG EXCREMENT ON PUBLIC PROPERTY. VIOLATORS WILL BE PROSECUTED. BY-LAW Nº 2017

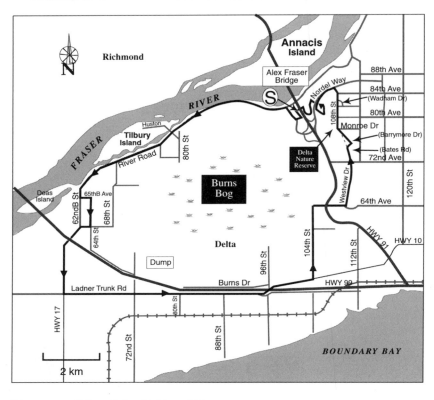

Distance and Elev Gain	33.8 km, 125 m, return
Terrain, Road, Traffic	flat, except hilly for the last 7 km; paved, with short section of trail; some quieter roads, with 24 km along busier highways and arterials that have bike routes or paved shoulders
Difficulty	F3 T4
Bike	gears suggested
Access	starting point favours cyclists coming S across the Alex Fraser Bridge along Hwy 91 "bike route"; otherwise, you could begin on River Road or at the (seasonal) drop-off point for the George Massey Tunnel shuttle on 62 B St at Hwy 99
Short Description	beginning along the Fraser River, this trip encircles ecologically unique Burns Bog, with a visit to attractive Deas Island Regional Pk

ROAD LOG

0.0   bicycle access at SW corner of Alex Fraser Bridge; head S and W on bike path

0.2   right on maintenance yard access road

0.4   right on Nordel Way

1.2   left on River Rd; **Caution: *dual paved shoulder attracts chunks of concrete and wood***

2.2   Sunbury School (decommissioned) on left — bog access via hogfuel trail at rear

2.4   9425 on right: Vito Steel Boat and Barge Construction

3.8   8828 on left: Delta Recycling Society

5.0   shingle mill on right

5.8   Huston Rd, right to cattail marsh and Dow-Delta fishing bar; for bog access turn left, then go right along 80th St through industrial area to wet pine forest

9.3   road divides

9.8   road becomes 62 B St; Deas Island Regional Pk access, open 8 am-dusk (9 pm in summer) washrooms, multi-bin recycling GVRD Parks (520-6442)

10.4   left on 65 B Ave; llamas and sheep on left

10.6   right on 64th St/Crescent Island Rd

11.8   right on 60th Ave (for landfill, go straight instead and follow bending road to end)

12.0   6201 on right: Chamber of Commerce (946-4232)

12.1   left on 62 B St

12.4   (seasonal) George Massey Tunnel shuttle on right

12.5   **Caution: *exiting/merging traffic***

13.0   cross two merging lanes to join Hwy 17

14.7   left on Hwy 10/Ladner Trunk Rd

21.6   left on overpass

22.2   on right: East Delta Church, 1891

22.4   Vandura farm and market on right: berries, etc.

23.7   left on 104th St/Kittson Rd

26.3   bog access on left; right on 64th Ave/Kittson Parkway

27.2   left on Westview Dr. (straight instead for Watershed Pk)

27.5   Westview Pk on right

28.9   right on 72nd Ave/Newton Rd

29.0   left on Blake Dr. (**Caution**); ignore "no through road" sign to pass two barriers

29.4   right uphill on Bates Rd (straight instead for Delta Nature Reserve)

29.5   left on Barrymore Dr.

30.3   angle right at Monroe Dr. onto 108th St

31.4   continue on trail at Wadham Dr.

31.6   left on 84th Ave/Richardson Rd (curb)

Who can resist watching the llamas?

Note: officially, cyclists are expected to get onto the SE sidewalk for the trip down the hill on Nordel Way; if you happen to end up going down with the traffic, get to the "bike route" by climbing over the concrete barrier just beyond the railway overpass and looking for a ramp down

32.3 left on Nordel Way (on sidewalk)
33.0 railway overpass
33.1 left on paved path to loop around beneath road
33.4 **Caution:** *occasional flooding and poor visibility*
33.8 access to E sidewalk of Alex Fraser Bridge; loop under bridge to get back to start
34.0 starting point
More information: Burns Bog Conservation Society, #203, 11961 88th Ave, Delta, BC, V4C 3C9, 572-0373

If you've lived in the Lower Mainland for awhile, you've probably heard of Burns Bog, but may not have given it much consideration as anything other than the site of a landfill somewhere in Delta. It used to be prized berry gathering terrain to native people, and it's also home to deer and bear, but it's even more special than that.

Burns Bog began forming around 5000 years ago when enough sediments collected in the Fraser delta that they broke the surface. Over time, brackish marshes developed, collecting yet more silt during high water. A dome shape eventually rose as an acidic peat bog formed. The unusual conditions here support not only sphagnum mosses but also many plants normally found high in the mountains or much further north, and several others not found anywhere else. Surrounding the central heathlands are rings dominated by stunted lodgepole pines, paper birch, and hardhack spireas.

An ancient barge—one of the many interesting sights along River Road.

There are several smaller bogs in the Fraser Valley, but Burns Bog is unique. According to Richard Hebda, a professor of biology at the University of Victoria, you won't find another bog this size with the same mix of species anywhere else in the world. The last hundred years of human activity have scarred, but not killed, the old bog. It had a close call though, in 1989, when only a great public outcry prevented it from being dredged for a superport. There is still an opportunity to preserve this ecological treasure, but it's important to protect all of it, and not just a piece of it, because the bog's components work together as an organic unit.

Several access points to Burns Bog are mentioned in the road log, but it's not wise to venture into the bog alone unless you know the area. In any case, keep to trails both to protect the bog vegetation and to avoid falling into a quagmire.

While riding along River Road, you'll find mostly fish and wood processing industries. (You may recognize a few buildings from Expo '86.) Highlights include boatworks and occasional cattail marshes, feeding areas for ducks and herons, and Deas Island Regional Park.

Deas Island (long since a peninsula) no longer betrays more than a trace of its history as the site of the most productive salmon cannery on the Fraser River for three years running. When he claimed the island and built the first cannery in 1873, John Sullivan Deas constructed the original dykes by hand; over the years they've been improved and extended.

If you visit Deas Island today, you'll find a park endowed with (relocated) historic buildings, grassy picnic areas, and pleasant, treed dyke-top walking trails meandering past low meadows and wooded marshes. The western end has a different character, consisting mostly of rapidly over-growing sand piles and seasonally flooded deciduous forest, with treed rocky lookouts guarding the tip. From the many river viewpoints (and a viewing platform) you can watch river traffic and maybe even see otters, muskrat, or seals.

On the rest of the loop, you pass mostly through farmland, but also through residential areas. You'll find roadside produce stands and U-pick farms along Hwy 10 and 104th St.

NEXT PAGE: Youngsters learn best if they're having fun.

The Many Faces of Cycling

Why do people ride bicycles? There are many reasons for mounting the saddle, taking the handlebars in hand, and setting off down the road or trail.

Remember to stop and smell the flowers along the way!

Recreational riders cycle for fun and fitness, to "get away from it all," to visit favourite haunts, or to explore new territory. You'll find them riding to the park five blocks over, on day trips, on cross-country tours, and out on the backwoods trails, cycling alone or in groups.

Competitive cyclists generally seek, with varying degrees of ferocity, to climb new pinnacles of physical prowess and skill, to better their own past performances, or to best others. Their excitement is to push their limits and those of their equipment, to set goals and achieve them. Other rewards come in the form of camaraderie and team spirit. Competitive cyclists ride on cycle tracks, on the road, on cyclocross courses, on rugged mountain trails, and on BMX courses.

Transportation or utility cycling, though less glamorous than the varieties mentioned above, has the most potential to beneficially change our lives through better health and reduced pollution. It includes commuting to work or school, grocery shopping, or visiting friends. Some people may ride a bike in the course of their employment: couriers, police officers, and newspaper carriers, for instance.

The following sections offer further insight into these uses.

RECREATIONAL RIDING

Recreational riders can be separated into two overlapping categories: those who cycle primarily for the physical fitness benefits, and those who choose the bicycle as their favourite way to experience their surroundings and explore new areas.

Cycling Is Good For You

The hours you spend cycling are not, as the Babylonians used to say of fishing, deducted from your allotted span. In fact, every hour of physical activity can add as much as 1 to 2.5 hours to your expected life span. Work by Dr Kenneth H. Cooper suggests that you need only ride 13 km at a moderate 25 km/h (about half an hour), three times per week, to maintain your cardiovascular system once you are in condition.

Cycling can also help keep you trim: riding on the level at 25 km/h, propelling a total mass of 80 kg (including yourself), burns about 350 calories per hour; more if you're heading uphill, travelling faster, catching some wind, or carrying extra weight. Compared to jogging or running, it's usually easier on your joints and shins (though riding in too high a gear may lead to knee problems).

Nature's Cycles

Cycle-touring can be a year-round activity if you're properly prepared. Summer offers the most freedom: a time for beaches and picnics, and for longer trips. However, the other seasons, too, have their special qualities. In the fall, choose a route with indoor highlights, or one that features autumn colours. The colder months are timely for a visit to Delta to see the great flocks of wintering waterfowl. Finally, spring is excellent for a tour of Vancouver or New Westminster, to enjoy the lovely explosion of blossoms on the street trees.

You can also take advantage of local variations in climate: though it might be raining in mountainous North Vancouver, it's frequently sunny on the delta lands of Richmond and Delta, where annual precipitation is less than half as much. And if it's too hot on the uplands, take advantage of the dependable breeze along the seashore.

Faster Isn't Always Better

The slower and closer to the ground you travel, the more detail you experience. From a jet you see only very large things; from a car, you perhaps see a little more; and on foot, you not only see the most but you smell and feel so much more of your environs, as well. The bicycle offers a good compromise while still allowing a reasonable degree of freedom in speed, course, and carrying capacity. In other words, on a bike you can speed up to conjure a cool, caressing breeze upon your heat-flushed cheeks, or turn down a side path to stop and smell the roses along the way, and then pull a nature guide out of your handlebar bag to identify the butterfly you just discovered.

What To Take On A Day Trip

When you have to carry it yourself, too much can be as bad as not enough. Though every cyclist has slightly different needs and priorities, consider selecting from the following items:

• safety gear: helmet, light, reflective vest

• tool kit (groups: to fit everyone's bike)

• suitable clothing, including wind/rain wear and perhaps walking shoes

• food and drink

• first aid supplies: bandages, disinfectant, pain reliever, etc.

• suntan lotion, insect repellent, prescription drugs, hygiene products

- quarters for phone calls; money for food, shopping, taxi, ferry, etc.

- maps, guidebooks, ferry schedules

- other goodies: camera and film, binoculars, sketch pad, frisbee, swimwear, flute, nature guides, toys and games for the children, etc.

Overnight Trips

Camping, at formal or informal sites, is a popular way to spend the night in rural and wilderness areas. It can add a lot to the experience, and gives more freedom in choosing route and pace. (It is polite to ask permission if you plan to camp, for instance, in a farmer's field and you might even be treated to dinner!) To reduce the amount of gear required, you may prefer to stay with friends or relatives, in a bed-and-breakfast, hostel, motel, or hotel. Some charismatic individuals even get along just fine by getting invited to stay with people they meet, but this technique carries no guarantees!

For longer trips, consider adding these items to those suggested for a day trip:

- sleeping bag and foam pad or similar

- tent and/or tarp

- cookstove & fuel (white gas recommended), matches, cooking pot, plate, cutlery, cup, seasonings, condiments, oil, etc.

- change(s) of clothes and footwear

- toiletries: soap, towel, toothbrush, toilet paper, etc.

- miscellaneous items: needle and thread, water purifier or chemicals, string, pocket flashlight, etc.

Packing For Touring

Frequently used items such as cameras, snacks, and guidebooks should be packed for ready access. Store anything that needs to stay dry in a waterproof stuffsack or plastic bag, firstly because panniers leak and secondly because you'll sometimes need to take something out while it's raining.

Experiments have shown that the most stable handling resulted when standard rear panniers were counterbalanced with low-mount front panniers. About 60% of the weight should be at the rear, and handlebar bags should be kept lightweight, or steering may be affected. Pack ahead of time and ride at least around the block to see how it feels; the load should balance well and not be too heavy.

Getting There

Of course it's less hassle if you can ride straight from your door, but sometimes you will feel like skipping over some of the urban roads or highways between you and the pleasanter parts. Public transit can sometimes fill the need (see the section *Getting Where You're Going*). Otherwise, if you have access to a truck or a van, you can simply lay the bike down or tie it upright. Some cars will take bikes in the trunk or the back seat (often you will have to remove a wheel) but a bike rack can preserve both your cargo space and your upholstery.

Rooftop racks don't interfere with access to the trunk, but make getting the bikes on and off more difficult and expose the bikes to risk from low-clearance branches, tunnels, etc. The trunk-mounting types are much easier to load and unload but the bikes are more vulnerable to dust and rocks from the road and may obscure your car's signal lights. In any case, make sure that your rack and bike can be securely locked to deter theft while you're gulping down a vegieburger at your favourite cafe.

Cycling In Good Company

Cycling with others gives opportunities to make and strengthen friendships, to share experiences and cycling know-how, and to provide mutual support. Breaks and meals are especially good for getting to know your companions. Larger touring groups give more choice in people to ride with and talk to, but are likely to become more self-contained, reducing the intensity of the experience of the territory you're riding through. Organizational challenges also increase with group size.

It's the attitude more than the equipment that makes a ride enjoyable.

Group harmony is especially important for longer trips, but even the shortest outing is more fun if everyone is treated with respect and understanding. Although it's common for groups to spread out according to their riding ability, no one should feel like a neglected straggler. This may mean asking stronger cyclists to take it easy and according them a greater share of the provisions to carry and regrouping at intervals at pre-arranged locations. An experienced cyclist who knows the route—equipped with tools, first aid supplies, and some extra food and water—should bring up the rear to make sure everyone succeeds.

Relative Harmony

The family that cycles together stays together, if everyone takes into account the needs and abilities of the others. Family cycling is a form of group cycling where you can't just say goodbye when the ride is over and things didn't work out. Communication is essential, especially if you ride on tandems. Fitter family members can remain popular by cycling at a pace that suits the less athletic, and encouraging sufficient rest breaks.

Babies can be quite happy in a child carrier or in a trailer, which is more easily balanced, but toddlers will demand to stop more often. Children who want to pedal but are too young to ride individual bikes can be accommodated with child-crank conversions that clamp onto the back seat tube of a tandem, or with a half-bike trailer. Bikes for older children should be selected and adjusted for a proper fit. Remember that no one you love is too young or too old to do without a helmet.

Respectable Distances, Respectable Times

Randonneurs are a group of recreational riders who might at first glance be mistaken for racers. They travel light and take their cycling seriously, yet still have time to be sociable. In BC, ride length varies from an early-season 200 km up to 1000 km. You don't need to be exceptionally fast to be a randonneur—average speeds between about 15 and 30 km/h are typical—but endurance is essential.

THE BICYCLE AS TRANSPORTATION

Why

Even in the wee hours of the morning, during half an hour of cycling major city streets you are almost sure to encounter several other cyclists. On a daytime ride you will discover dozens; such are the numbers and commitment to this form of transportation. (A 1985 study of the Vancouver Central Metropolitan Area found that over 47 000 bicycle trips were made on an average weekday.) Why do so many people choose to commute to work and school, visit, or run errands by bicycle instead of by car or public transit? Here are some of the compelling reasons why people exercise the self-propelled two-wheel transportation option:

Convenience: Bicycle parking (often informal) is usually available closer to where you need to be than it is for a car, without lineups. Bicycles don't need warming up or defogging before use, either. They outshine transit especially if you have several stops to make.

Cost: Bicycle purchase, maintenance, and repair costs are less than for an automobile. (Repairing a dented panel on a car can cost more than a new bicycle!) Insurance and parking are also cheaper. In addition, each car costs society at least $2750 yearly in subsidies (Dr William Rees cited in *From Desolation to Hope: The Pacific Fraser Region in 2010*). Cycling to work can save you even more if your employer has a fitness or environmental program with cash rewards for commuter cyclists.

Environmental Concerns: Bicycles are undeniably more environmentally sound than automobiles or even public transit. According to the *Canadian Green Consumer Guide*, bicycles boast 10 times the efficiency (in passenger-kilometres per unit of energy) of city buses and 40 times the efficiency of cars. Every car replaced with a bicycle means fewer natural areas despoiled by oil drilling or by spills. Cars are also the major contributor to urban-runoff pollution in Georgia Strait. In addition, while even a small car ties up perhaps 1000 kg of materials in its construction, a bike gets by with less than 15 kg. A bicycle also has much more modest road and parking space needs. (In Vancouver, for example, 25% of the land area is already occupied by roads.) Finally, a typical car produces an average annual 1637 kg (BC Transit's *Transit and the Environment*, 1990) of atmospheric pollutants (contributing to acid rain, the greenhouse effect, and health problems) whereas a bike produces none, and makes far less noise besides.

Fitness and Training: If you wouldn't otherwise have time for regular aerobic exercise, or for training for weekend racing, you can get it almost for free by trading in car or bus travel time.

Mental Well-being: By avoiding traffic jams you reduce stress and arrive invigorated with a general feeling of well-being. Cycling is also more conducive to a spirit of community than is the isolating cocoon of the automobile. You're much more aware of what's happening in your neighbourhood, the changes in the weather, and the cycles of plant and animal life that mark the changing seasons.

Speed: Travel by bicycle (especially for shorter trips in urban areas) can often be even faster than by car because of parking considerations and because you can bypass traffic jams, and faster than by bus because your bike is ready to go when you are (no transfers needed!) and doesn't stop to pick up and drop off other people.

Where

Which to use, the main roads or the side roads? For the experienced cyclist in a hurry, the arterials are almost always faster, though they aren't much fun during rush hour. Unquestionably, however, secondary roads will be more relaxing, and expose you to less pollution, less noise, and less potential risk. Dr Lorne Whitehead of the Vancouver Bikeways Network Group compared a trip down Vancouver's Broadway with one along 14th Avenue: on the former he counted 250 trees and 600 cars; on the latter 1100 trees and only two cars! He also pointed out that the greater number of cars and higher speeds on Broadway leave less room for error, with worse possible consequences.

By varying your route from day to day, you can discover all kinds of neat things you didn't know existed.

How

Once you've decided to use your bike for transportation, appropriate clothing and other equipment are especially important if you plan to continue cycling through the colder, wetter, darker months (see *Nuts, Bolts, and Cloth*).

Commuters often either pack a change of clothing with them or have it waiting at their destinations. If you're lucky, you will have (or be able to arrange) secure parking and showers at or near your destination. If you have to do without showers, take it easy on the way in and get your big workout on your way home.

MOUNTAIN BIKES: FRESH HORIZONS FOR CYCLING

New Kid On The Block

Over the years, hikers and equestrians have gained levels of acceptance with provincial and municipal land managers as legitimate trail users; many trails have been constructed and maintained for and by these users. However, mountain bikers have yet to earn widespread recognition of this kind. The largest provincial umbrella group for hikers and mountaineers goes so far as to state that "the Federation of Mountain Clubs is opposed to the use of mountain bikes on trails traditionally intended for hiking," and then goes on to suggest that mountain-biking groups construct their own appropriately designed trails.

While dyke trails are mostly open to cyclists, there are as yet only a few tentative officially sanctioned routes of a more varied and challenging nature: for example, the Old Buck Trail on Mount Seymour, and the BLT Trail on Cypress. Many other trails are explicitly closed to cyclists, with the possibility of fines for those who use them. Logging roads only partially fill the gap: active ones are often closed weekdays and usually lack challenge while abandoned ones have frequently degenerated into tiresome boulder fields. In response to the lack of suitable venues to practice their chosen sport, riders have indeed begun to take the initiative to create their own trails. Mostly building informally and discreetly, they are not bound by the standards and liability concerns restricting the municipal and provincial park authorities.

Ross Kirkwood is one local aficionado who has dedicated thousands of hours to trail building and maintenance over the last ten years. He has refined his techniques to maximize the fun factor of a trail while minimizing damage to the terrain. Water erosion, for instance, can be significantly reduced through the judicious use of switchbacks and the avoidance (or gravel in-filling) of wet spots. However, probably the most important factor in trail maintenance is educating riders to take responsibility for their share, to pause a moment to fix a little problem or to come out for a work party; the old saying "many hands make light work" sums it up.

If you live in Vancouver and feel like doing some mountain bike exploring but don't have time to get out of the city, take to the alleys. There are some dandy ones that the paving crews haven't yet discovered, especially in the southwestern part of the city. If you do have more time, mountain biking is popular in the Whistler area (there is a trail handbook available), or you could head off into the back country on logging roads (check with the Ministry of Forests for maps and safety information).

Why Did They Close That Trail?

In previous years, cyclists would ride up the old gravel Grouse Mountain Highway back route to Grouse Mountain Resort. To prevent unfortunate collisions between their guests and bikers, resort personnel signposted the paved resort paths as "no cycling." They also asked riders not to bring their bikes onto the bistro deck, and installed a bike rack at the edge of their resort area. Because these requests went unheeded by too many cyclists, and because of a liability concern prompted by several serious accidents on the access road, cyclists are now unwelcome at the resort and on the road. A deep rift has been created between frustrated mountain bikers and exasperated resort management. This is an unfortunate case in point where some cyclists riding without concern for the sensitivities of others has led to all cyclists being banned from an area where they were previously tolerated.

In the USA, where mountain-biking is more established, many choice trails are being placed off limits to cyclists. In BC the sport is younger and there is perhaps still time for it to mature with a good reputation.

While many mountain bikers believe that both land managers and the general public would be more accepting of off-road cycling if only they understood the sport better, most serious cyclists also feel it's everyone's duty to ride responsibly. If you ride off-road for the exhilaration of powering through streams or cleaning gnarly hill-trails in record time, do it where any damage you cause will be minimal, and pick times and places where you're unlikely to traumatize hikers or horse riders. By respecting other trail users and land owners/managers, you gain respect and acceptance not just for yourself but for the whole cycling community.

Devastating Descents, Heartbreaking Hillclimbs

When it's time to test the limits of your skills and fitness, that's when you take up racing. Although the mountain bike was originally developed for downhill racing, other events have been growing in popularity. In BC, riders participate in downhill, hill climb, and criterium (multiple laps of a less technical course) races, but the cross-country event is the most popular. A big competition can draw 200–300 participants.

Successful cross-country racing demands good technique and a high level of fitness. You need all the gears, including the "two foot" gear (pushing or carrying your bike). Riders in the men's "expert" category can face 20 to 40 km of devastating descents and heartbreaking hillclimbs through mud and sand, over rocks and logs. Competitors in the other men's categories (sportsman, novice, junior) and the women's categories (expert, novice) are challenged proportionately.

Competitions have been staged (usually with special permission) on Burnaby Mountain, on Mt Seymour, on Grouse Mountain, at Cypress, along Mosquito Creek, on Vedder Mountain, and in the Squamish-Whistler area. Other venues are in the Okanagan and on Vancouver Island.

Though you can get a bike that will stand up to off-road racing conditions for about $700, a top-of-the-line model can set you back $3500. Even then, rims and derailleurs are common casualties. The cash prizes awarded at bigger races help, but many competitors above the novice category enter into a symbiotic relationship with a bike shop sponsor; the racers get discounts on their equipment and the sponsor gets publicity.

Many people are either fit or have good technique, but it takes dedicated training to excel at both. For example, Trish Sinclair, who races on the Robson Cycles team, competes almost every weekend from March to October, commutes to work by bike, and still makes time for three additional training rides throughout the week. Her efforts paid off with first place in the women's expert category in both the 1991 BC Off-Road Championship and the 1991 Okanagan Series.

For Trish and many other off-road racers, it isn't necessarily the glory of winning that keeps them in the sport, however. They enjoy challenging their personal limits and being out in the wilderness, off the paved roads, and in the good-spirited company of like-minded folk.

To find out more about mountain bike racing, inquire at your local bike shop or the Bicycling Association of BC.

Riding Responsibly:

• *Slow down (possibly stop or walk) when passing other trail users. Be courteous. Give pedestrians and equestrians the right-of-way, and call out a friendly greeting or ring your bell, especially if approaching from behind. Avoid spooking horses by leaving plenty of room when passing; pass or wait on the low side of the trail if possible.*

• *Ride where your passage will not leave signs objectionable to others: hard dirt trails, gravel, etc. Don't ride through alpine meadows and other fragile ecosystems.*

• *Respect no cycling signs; their use is usually an honest attempt to protect you, other trail users, wildlife, or the trail itself from injury or disturbance. (If you feel they aren't justified, phone the appropriate land manager to talk about it.)*

• *Give soft soils a few days to dry after a rain before riding on them.*

• *Control your speed so you don't end up locking the back wheel and tearing up the ground on every bend.*

• *Ride single file to leave manoeuvring room for you and anyone you might meet.*

• *Ride on the high part of the trail instead of deepening the ruts.*

• *Help to maintain the trails you use. For info on trail building/maintenance, call the BABC, or write to Ross Kirkwood, Secret Trails Society, Main PO Box 3292, Vancouver, B.C., V6B 3X9*

THE RACING SCENE

"Coming down a really narrow mountain road at 60 miles an hour [97 km/h] is just an incredible thrill...when you're sitting right on the yellow line, and just zooming down, and you know you can pass anything that's on the road because your cornering on a bike is just incredible compared to any other vehicle. I become part of the bike and the bike becomes part of me," explains Vancouver racer Peter Aram to illustrate his fascination with road racing. In *Effective Cycling*, John Forester describes bicycle racing in general as "one of the most demanding sports in the world," requiring a singular "combination of strength, power, endurance, control, and intelligence."

The romance of bicycle racing has its roots in the days of the high-wheeler (now also called an ordinary or penny-farthing), when professional cyclists were paid by competing manufacturers to demonstrate the excellence of their respective products. Track racing began in 1869. Racing came to Vancouver just after the founding of the city and caught on quickly. The first race is believed to have been on Water Street, which was then planked rather than cobbled. Brockton Oval was constructed for cycle racing and was used for many professional events during the 1890s, though it is now used for baser purposes. The wooden China Creek Cycle Bowl track, a legacy from the 1954 British Empire and Commonwealth Games, was carefully restored in 1973, but by the end of the decade it had been torn down to make way for the King Edward Campus of Vancouver Community College.

Track training helps build the sprinting and manoeuvring skills necessary for successful road racing, so the China Creek track was sadly missed by all racers. In the years before the (projected) 1992 opening of the Harry Jerome Sports Centre velodrome, ardent BC cyclists would have to go to Redmond, Washington, for track time. On a typical summer weekend they'd log some 500 car kilometres driving down on Friday night and returning in time for Sunday road races.

Vancouver is Canada's road-racers' paradise. Even part of the national team trains here because the temperate climate allows year-round workouts. Interval sprints and endurance rides are done on regular roads; popular areas are in Richmond, Delta, Pitt Meadows-Maple Ridge, Glen Valley, Hatzic Valley, Sumas Prairie, and Matsqui Prairie. A longer club ride might be from downtown Vancouver to Chilliwack and back, covering 150 km in 6–8 hours. Hill-climbing practice is also close at hand, on roads leading to nearby mountains: Seymour, Cypress, Whistler, and Baker. Competitive techniques are honed at club meets.

Traditional bicycle racing falls into three categories: track, criterium, and road. Track events are typically the shortest—with the outcome often resolved in just a few seconds—and come in the greatest variety: some 15 different events. A special bike is used, with a fixed gear (about 5:1) and no brakes (you slow down by resisting the turning of the pedals). On indoor tracks, without headwinds or hills, racers can often coax average speeds of over 50 km/h out of their 6.5 kg bikes.

Criterium races take place on short courses (under 1 km in Canada) with sharp corners. The many (50 or so) laps allow stationary spectators to keep ongoing track of the action. "Primes" (bonuses of points, bagels, beer, cash, etc.) are awarded for certain laps to prompt exciting sprints and maintain spectator interest.

Road races are longer events, starting around 90 km in March and progressing to over 130 km by the season's end in September (for men; 50 km-80 km for women). Each lap is typically 15 km long and often includes at least one steep hill. Stage races are multi-day road races, usually in different locations, with combined point totals. Time trials, which range from 0.5 to 100 km, are perhaps more pure in that they pit the individual or the team against the terrain without the advantages and disadvantages of having competitors around.

Many types of races are run as team events, allowing club members to work together to execute more powerful and exciting strategies than they could if they were competing individually.

Most racers today join clubs because membership can provide camaraderie, support, and the opportunity to learn from more experienced riders and coaches; (often) sponsorship by a bicycle store or manufacturer, resulting in lower costs for bikes and transportation; and lower license fees.

Licensing is controlled by the BABC. Beginners start with a novice card (mandatory for senior men) or a license for cat (category) 4 in cadet, junior, senior, or veteran age-classes in the men's or women's divisions. They move up to cats 3, 2, and 1 based on their performance or by special application. Though some racers attain cat 1 in a single season, others are happy to stay in cat 4.

Two points troubling some members of the local racing community are an increase in the number of racers proudly riding the hottest new bikes but without any technical understanding, and the emergence of a European-style elitism. They feel cycling could be a much stronger and more appealing sport if everyone embraced a more holistic, egalitarian approach.

CYCLOCROSS

"It's just plain fun. You have to take everything that happens with a very big grain of salt, because anything can happen. You can hit a log and break your wheel...and the mud makes it even more fun because you're slipping and sliding and falling down," says a local cyclocross participant. Minor bruises and scrapes are common occurrences as well, he concedes.

To get an image of what cyclocross is like, imagine a steeplechase, but replace the horses with bikes and add lots more mud. The prepared courses used for cyclocross are short: 3 or 4 km total length covered in five laps, for example. Obstacles—including mud holes, fences, sharp zig-zags, and impossibly steep slopes—mean that a participant will sometimes have to push or carry the bike through half the course.

A cyclocross bike is much like a road-racing bike, but has somewhat wider knobby tires, and only six to eight speeds. Unlike mountain bike racing, a cyclocross competitor is permitted a fresh bike every lap. There are separate mass starts for each category—women (about 15% of the starting lineup), junior men (30%) and senior men (remainder)—with modest prizes for each.

By European standards, cyclocross in BC has a fairly small following, but to the devoted, the first race of the season is a sure sign that fall has arrived.

RECKLESS DAREDEVILS OR MISUNDERSTOOD TALENTED PROFESSIONALS?

Within their domain, no street nor alley escapes their passage, no bank nor office tower the sound of their footsteps. Every sense alert for possible hazards, muscles straining to beat the clock, they skilfully navigate through the bustling downtown core. Individualistic yet sociable, drawn to their way of life by a love of cycling, they are bicycle couriers.

Bicycle messengers date from the era of the telegraph delivery boy, but over time the need for this service faded. Car couriers had been around for some time when someone realized that short trips through grid-locked city centres could be better handled by cyclists. This phenomenon spread to Vancouver in 1982. Today there are approximately a dozen companies in the city offering bike courier service, and some 500 (annually) licensed couriers. You will only see about 75 on the road at any given time, however, for there is a high turnover rate. Novices often decide to seek their fortunes elsewhere after a couple months, but there is a solid core of three-to-five year veterans. Ages range from late teens to forties, with women accounting for two of every five riders.

Being a bicycle courier is by no means easy. You have to enjoy working with your body, use it properly, and be sensitive to joints that need a rest. Whatever the weather, you're out there riding. You must continually be aware of your position in the complex ebb and flow of traffic and pedestrians. Finally, there's the pressure to perform: most couriers are paid by the piece, and the competition for jobs is fierce. As a courier, you're an independent contractor and your relationship with the dispatcher can affect both the number and quality of your assignments. If it's a good day, you might manage 40 to 50 trips averaging four blocks each, all within the narrow limits of the downtown business core, but you may not get a chance to eat properly.

Aggressive, second-shaving riding techniques attributed to the commission system brought about complaints from other road users and pedestrians. In response, the city and the BABC co-developed a licensing system that requires prospective couriers to demonstrate through a written exam and a road test their ability to ride safely and legally. Most couriers like the program because it confirms them as legitimate and professional users of the road.

As committed "bicycle people," seasoned cycle couriers have a lot of information to share with other riders. In trying to corner a courier, though, make sure you pick a quiet day. Good places to look are "Biker Beach" (aka the steps of the old court house on Robson Street) and Starbuck's Coffee outlets. Once they warm to the topic, couriers will gladly share with you their tales of woe and misery. More positively, they also possess a firsthand knowledge of urban riding techniques and cycling equipment. (Although a few use cheap clunker bikes and some choose road bikes, most ride high quality mountain bikes for durability and stability.) After all, when you spend your work day straddling a saddle and go through a bike every year or two, you learn a few things.

A FEW NOTES ON SUCCESSFUL CYCLING

Even if you're an experienced cyclist, please skim through this section in case there's something you've forgotten or never knew.

Living With Traffic

Contrary to what some novice cyclists believe, most cycling accidents do not involve a car; many are falls, or collisions with pedestrians, trees, dogs, and even other cyclists. When a car-bike accident does occur, the cause is often poor cycling skills.

It's up to you as a cyclist to ride where drivers have learned to look, and to act predictably, in accordance with the rules set out for operators of vehicles (or, if walking the bike, with those applying to pedestrians). It's also important to choose clothing and other equipment that will make you readily visible, especially in the rain and at night. Finally, keep alert and be prepared to take evasive action if a driver doesn't yield when you expect. Just in case somebody goofs, always wear a helmet to reduce the chance of head injuries.

How Far Right? • Don't ride as far right as possible. Ride far enough left to avoid tempting drivers to pass where there isn't enough space, to be out of reach of doors opening on parked cars, to avoid hitting your pedal on the curb, to avoid dangerous loose gravel or debris, and to allow you to see pedestrians and vehicles entering from the right. The poorer the road/traffic/visibility conditions and the faster you are travelling, the closer to the left car wheel-track of your lane you need to be. Also, don't blindly weave back and forth to hug the curb between parked cars; only move right if you'll be riding there for a reasonable amount of time (or briefly to let something go by).

Being Passed And Getting Pastn • Many motorists will come up behind you and be uncertain whether or not to pass. Be a good sport: look back to acknowledge the car's presence and/or signal for it to pass when it is safe to do so.

When a truck or bus approaches to pass, you can reduce its wind effects on you by riding farther to the right, pedalling faster in a lower gear, and keeping a low, aerodynamic profile.

Even if you don't think there's anything behind you when you plan to swerve, look first; there could be another cyclist silently trying to overtake you. Conversely, when passing other cyclists, be sure to give them the benefit of a warning and/or lots of space.

You aren't supposed to pass on the right side of traffic in your lane. This hardly seems fair when you consider the number of cars that will pass a cyclist coming up to a red light; some experts suggest that you can pass with caution as long as you don't interfere with the first car in the lineup.

Crossing Busy Streets • *At a traffic light*, look for a pedestrian push button. If there isn't one, the light should change automatically. Otherwise, centre your bike over the traffic sensor if there is one (look for telltale wires in pavement; call city hall if this doesn't work), wait for a car to trigger a sensor, or resort to the push button and either return to the road or walk across on the crosswalk.

If there is no traffic light, the safest option is to wait patiently for a large enough gap to open, through chance or kindness. Otherwise, if you feel confident dealing with traffic, you can often encourage drivers to stop, but make sure that they have ample opportunity to do so, and carefully watch all lanes, especially those hidden by vehicles that have already stopped. It helps if you walk your bike, and wave thanks (this also makes you easier to notice), but don't assume that people will necessarily stop until they do.

Turning Left • Depending on traffic density, you could turn left with traffic from the rightmost left turn lane; ride straight through, stop, and then resume in the new direction when the lights change; or walk with the pedestrian lights, in whichever order they turn in your favour. Beware of intersections with one or two closed crosswalks.

Do Cyclists Need To Signal? • Under the Motor Vehicle Act you are required to signal left and right turns and stops. If you don't signal, you mislead other road users. Often this creates only an inconvenience to others, but it can also cost you in injuries and fines.

When turning or avoiding obstacles, look over your shoulder to see if it's safe, signal, look again, then make your move.

Unsigned Intersections And Four-Way Stops • Intersections with neither stop signs nor signals are called courtesy stops. Approach with care; whoever gets to the intersection first has the right-of-way. If it's a tie, the person on your right has precedence.

Four-way stops are like unsigned intersections but in practice whoever has been waiting longest at the stop line (not including time spent behind!) generally goes next. However, opposite cars will often go through simultaneously if both are going straight and right turns occur whenever there's an opening, so signalling is especially important. Eye contact and use of gestures help resolve uncertainties.

NEXT PAGE: Many cyclists feel safer on arterials if there is a bike lane.

When a traffic light breaks down, the intersection should be treated as a four-way stop, but in reality traffic often goes through in groups whenever the drivers think they can get away with it; use care.

Don't just cruise right through unsigned intersections and four-way stops: though you might get away with it for a while, you could run smack! into someone equally reckless.

Traffic circles (roundabouts to the British) are becoming common in Greater Vancouver. Always go around them to the right (counterclockwise) and otherwise treat them as courtesy stops.

Drivers To Watch: Some Danger Points • Occupied vehicles along the curb, in a driveway, or on a side road may pull out if the driver misjudges your speed or doesn't see you; ride further out (anything behind you?) and be prepared to stop or go around.

Avoid remaining in (or near) a driver's blind spot — in particular the right-rear side of the vehicle — especially when approaching intersections. For buses and transport trucks, this zone can extend over 20 metres behind the vehicle and into the lane to their right.

Beware the driver who passes and then turns right in front of you to cut you off. If this happens, use care if you decide to go around to the left. There may be something coming right behind. Otherwise turn sharply right with the car.

Watch for impatient oncoming drivers seeking to turn left, in case they decide to cross your path.

Be alert for vehicles slipping out of their lanes or otherwise crowding you, especially on curves or where the lane narrows.

Hazards Of The Road And Trail

Road edges and paved shoulders may harbour potholes and also collect debris: mufflers, wood, glass, gravel, etc. Shards from broken bottles are more damaging to tires than "road diamonds," the tempered glass cubes created when car windows break. Patches of sand or gravel can appear anywhere, especially at intersections and gravel driveways, and can cause loss of control. Keep alert and avoid these obstacles if practical, but sometimes it's safer to tackle them rather than swerve out into traffic.

Watch out for kite strings too!

To make a sudden turn to avoid an obstacle, first turn briefly towards it, then lean to turn away from it (practice). When braking sharply, keep your weight low and back and use your rear brake along with the more powerful front brake to avoid flying over the handlebars (a "header"), especially when going downhill. Brake before entering curves, rather than in them, because a braking wheel skids more easily. If you must brake in a curve, use the rear brake, not the front one.

Bumps are easier to negotiate if you put more of your weight on your pedals and less on your seat and handlebars. Develop your sense of dynamic balance: learn to shift your centre of gravity backwards and forwards again when going over a bump so as to keep most of your weight on the wheel that's not hitting the bump. Edges and slopes (small curbs, ruts) are best crossed at right angles. If you catch some air, land on the rear wheel.

Trails And Sidewalks • Riding on the sidewalk is unfair to pedestrians, who will not expect you to be there, unless it's part of a signed bicycle route. If you need to use a regular sidewalk or crosswalk, walk your bike. When meeting pedestrians, equestrians, or other cyclists on a shared way, move over to the right prior to meeting (unless signs or circumstances direct otherwise). If space is tight, cyclists should yield to pedestrians or equestrians, and to cyclists approaching from uphill. If approaching another person from behind, ring your bell or call out a greeting or an "excuse me, please." Slow down in any case, and be prepared to stop.

> • *Don't wear headphones while cycling: not only does it reduce your enjoyment of chirping birds and crickets, but the music might block the sound of approaching vehicles at a critical moment; besides, it can cost you a $75 fine.*
>
> • *If you feel you or your child could benefit from instruction in cycling in traffic or off-road, contact the BABC.*
>
> *"Unfortunately, most car-bike collisions are caused by cyclists of low skill committing the most elementary kinds of mistakes: disobeying the law, which implies a very low level of skill in traffic cycling."*
>
> *(Forester 1984, 152)*

Railroads • Right-angle railway crossings can be bumpy on skinny tires, but it's the diagonal crossings that can buck you off your saddle by diverting your front wheel. (Hence perhaps the name "cross-buck" for the railway sign!) Depending on your bike and experience, the traffic, the space available, and the degree of hazard, either stop and walk across; slow down, check traffic, signal a turn, and cross at right angles; or trust your finely-honed instincts to carry you safely through. (Even if you don't fall, the jarring can still cause your luggage to go flying.) The concrete crossings used for the coal train line to Robert's Bank are among the worst. Rubber flanges could be fitted to make crossings safer, but the railroads still need to be persuaded to do so at most locations.

Rainy Day Dangers • Roads become especially slick after a dry spell as accumulated oils are set free. Beware of metal plates, too. Take corners more slowly, and brake sooner and more gently to avoid locking up your wheels.

Drivers do not see as well through their rain-streaked, fogged-up windows. Like you, drivers will have less control of their vehicles. Give them a wider berth, dress visibly, and ride more cautiously in traffic.

Finally, if your clothing gets wet, just hanging around on a cold or windy day can bring on hypothermia. If you don't have extra clothing, take breaks out of the wind, or keep moving to generate heat.

Ice And Snow •(As for rain, only more so.) Get out the wide, knobby tires, or even tire chains. Fresh, untrammelled snow can be fun. Soft slush is mostly just bothersome. Breakable crust is nearly impossible. Frozen slush and icy ruts are treacherous, especially when covered by new snow. Flat ice can be tricky, even on foot. On slopes, it's worse. Every time it snows in Greater Vancouver, cars and trucks start sliding down the hills sideways and backwards. Stay home, wait for the traffic to clear, walk, take the bus, ski, or take a different route. Keep an eye on what's going on behind you and on the side streets ahead; anticipate trouble and get out of the way.

After an exhilarating journey through slush or snow, brush or wipe the souvenirs off your bike before they melt (leaving dirty salt water all over) or freeze solid.

Tips For Gravel Roads And Off-Road Riding • On loose gravel, look for a firmer track where other users have thinned the offending material. Be careful on turns in sand, gravel or mud, as your wheels will have a tendency to slide out from under you.

If you stop (or fall) on a narrow cycling trail, move over to the side to avoid being hit by other cyclists, especially where visibility is poor or terrain is steep or tricky.

Depending on where you ride you might be challenged by slippery clay, wood, and rock; sharp roots, stumps, and metal (frayed cables, nails, barbed wire, etc.); overhanging branches that obstruct your vision, bash you in the forehead, or shred your skin; twigs that spring through your wheels; stairs, boulders, holes, and washouts. Also watch out for pedestrians, other cyclists, bears, logging trucks, cliffs, etc. that might appear unexpectedly in front of you. If you know you can't stop in time, go around. If you must crash, choose a pond or a soft young conifer to land in.

> *It is the part of a wise man [or woman] to keep himself safe to-day for to-morrow, and not to adventure himself wholly in one day.*
> *-Sancho Panza, faithful servant to Don Quixote*
>
> *(Cervantes)*

With experience you will learn how to handle these obstacles. Until your skill and confidence develop, save yourself and others from bodily injury and damaged equipment by walking your bike where you don't feel comfortable riding. Bear in mind that twenty minutes of cycling can turn into two hours of pushing or carrying if you break your bike, and even more of an ordeal if you injure yourself. Take this into account especially if you're not prepared for night travel or are on your own. Keep your speed within your capabilities, especially on downslopes in unfamiliar terrain. Learn from others.

The Dog: Friend Or Foe? • Man's (or woman's) best friend can make cycling difficult, especially if the dog is someone else's. Even a friendly (but stupid or inexperienced) canine can cause trouble just by getting in the way. Worse are the over-protective dogs and vicious dogs. Of course the owners are to blame for not training and restraining them properly. You can make complaints to the bylaw enforcement officer of the jurisdiction where an incident occurs, or to the police if there are injuries; owners can be held legally responsible for the actions of their pets.

The best reaction to a hostile dog varies with the situation. Most dogs bark worse than they bite. Some can be befriended while others respond to a firm, commanding voice telling them to go home, sit, etc. Summoning the owner sometimes works. If you're a powerful rider, you might be able to outrun the dog — it'll probably give up after a few hundred metres. Though a few squirts from a water bottle can dampen a dog's excitement, kicking at it often has the opposite effect. Other attackers have been vanquished with hefty bike pumps. There are even tales of pursuing dogs being bought off with lunch leftovers. If you're faced with an incorrigible and obviously bloodthirsty adversary, use your bike and/or luggage as a shield and retreat or move past as you are able, meanwhile hoping for assistance.

Basic Principles

• Safe and enjoyable cycling derives from the principle of respect: for pedestrians, for other road users, for your bicycle, and for yourself.

• Respect for pedestrians means accepting their right to the use of sidewalks, and giving them the opportunity to cross the road safely.

• Respect for other road users means riding on the appropriate part of the road, being visible, looking before changing speed or direction and then signalling your intentions in advance, and letting faster ones pass if it is safe.

• Respect for your bicycle means treating it as if you plan to keep it, lubricating the chain and bearings, tightening loose parts, and inflating the tires properly.

• Respect for yourself means all these, and in addition: dressing according to the weather, having reasonable expectations, wearing a helmet, and giving injuries a chance to heal.

Accidents • If you're involved in an accident, first do what can be done to minimize the risk of further injuries, then summon the police (especially if there are injuries or damage) and ambulance (if there are serious injuries or potential head injuries). Take names, addresses, phone numbers, and license-plate and drivers-license numbers (where applicable) from those involved and from witnesses. Avoid discussing the accident with the other party(ies) lest you say something that might be interpreted to your disadvantage if the case goes to court.

You can seek damages from a guilty motorist through his or her insurance policy but be aware that recompense may be several months away. Also note that cyclists too have been held responsible for damage and injuries; you may want to consider liability insurance yourself (available e.g. through BABC).

Three Good Reasons For Not Riding Against Traffic

1. The speed of impact is the sum of your speed and that of the car you run into; potential for damage and injury increases with the square of the speed of impact.

2. Drivers, cyclists, and pedestrians crossing your path won't know to look for you coming.

3. You risk colliding with the legitimate cyclists whose road space you will be occupying.

BEING FRIENDS WITH YOUR BODY

Be Kind To Your Joints And Muscles

Just because your body remembers how to balance on a bike doesn't mean that it's in shape. Work up to longer rides, and pace yourself, especially if you haven't done much cycling for a few months. If you haven't been getting regular aerobic exercise, or if you have a medical condition, consult your doctor before doing any intensive cycling. Even if your cardiovascular system is in good condition from running or some other exercise, your cycling muscles might not be.

When approaching a hill or cycling into the wind, shift down before your cadence (pedal strokes per minute) drops significantly. Keeping up a good cadence is easier on your knees and more efficient. Try for 80 or higher; racers usually exceed 100. Climbing a hill standing up at a lower cadence uses different muscles but does take more energy than spinning your pedals in a lower gear.

Stay more comfortable by keeping your shoulder, neck, and head muscles relaxed. On trips over an hour, it also helps to periodically stretch/flex your neck, shoulders, arms, fingers, back and even your legs either off your bike or while riding (when there is no traffic).

If nerve or joint pains develop, correct the situation before permanent damage occurs. If your usual doctor is unable to help you with cycling-related injuries or other problems, get a referral to a sports medicine expert at one of the universities or in private practice.

Bread And Water Or Cake And Wine?

Runners call it hitting the wall, cyclists call it getting the bonk, or bonking. It means that your body has depleted its immediately available energy stores. Bonking weakens you physically, affects your judgement, and saps your spirit as well. Avoid this situation by eating properly, especially on more strenuous trips.

Eat before setting out but allow an hour or two for large meals to digest before riding. Emphasize complex carbohydrates (potatoes, pasta, rice) over fats and proteins. While riding, snack on fruit, cookies, granola bars, etc. for simple carbohydrates. Note that liquid carbohydrates from fruit juices and commercial energy formulas take effect in under half an hour while solid food can take over an hour.

Dehydration robs your strength and can cause light-headedness, headaches, and chills, so it's equally important to maintain your body's water content. Choose water and dilute drinks, not alcohol, and drink frequently rather than in large quantities.

NUTS, BOLTS, AND CLOTH

This section will answer some basic questions about equipment and clothing. For more information, talk to other cyclists and bike shop staff, and read other books and magazines.

Choosing The Best Bike

The mountain bike, or all-terrain bike (ATB), is currently the steed of choice for many, whether or not they ever leave the pavement. In selecting an ATB over its swifter cousin, the road bike, for use on paved roads, you compromise on hand positions, aerodynamics, weight, and tire drag. However, you gain an upright riding position, greater flat resistance, and superior stability and durability when faced with gravel, sloughed-off car parts, rough pavement, and even curbs. Off-road, the greater durability, wider range of gears, more reliable braking, and higher traction tires of the ATB have become essential.

Complicating the issue, there is a compromise: the hybrid bike. Going under various names, it purports to be a cross between the sleek racer and the sturdy mountain bike. With its typically upright riding position and intermediate tire width, it's often a good choice for the commuter or the casual recreational cyclist.

Even the hybrid can't be all things to all people. If you're excited by speed and distance on the macadam, get a racing or touring style bike (or perhaps a sleek recumbent); if thoughts of backcountry trails and logging roads quicken your pulse, get a mountain bike. One final thought: even the most expensive bike you can afford isn't the best if it doesn't fit or doesn't do what you want, or if fear of theft keeps it indoors. (And if you've got a trusty one-speed or three-speed that you're happy with, that's fine, too.)

New bikes can be bought at a bike shop, at a department store, or by mail order. Used bikes can be bought from friends or through classified ads, message boards, garage sales, police auctions, pawn and second-hand stores, rental outlets, and bike shops, but check them carefully for damage that could be expensive to repair.

What To Look For On A Bike

Bikes with up to 24 speeds are now readily available. Do you really need this many? Probably not. Do make sure that the lowest gear gives you enough torque for the slopes you intend to climb (taking into account your strength, weight, and packing habits) and that the highest gear allows you to cruise at a satisfactory speed with a reasonable cadence; the others should give you well-proportioned steps in between.

If you cycle more than occasionally, it's worth buying a bike with long-wearing components and parts. This is especially important for items such as rims (get good quality durable alloy ones that will work reliably even when wet), brakes, and derailleurs.

Narrow, almost smooth tires are the most efficient on pavement, but fat knobby tires will perform best on rough, steep, muddy, or loose-surface rides. The former will usually be found on road bikes and the latter on the ATB, but there is some leeway for each. Higher air pressure gives a more efficient ride while softer tires have more grip and absorb bumps better. (Note: underinflation can lead to damaged tires and rims.)

Fenders will keep your clothes cleaner. Some are designed for off-road use and/or easy installation and removal.

A seat is something you should choose carefully, to make sure it will still be comfortable at the end of a day's outing. Try rental bikes and friends' bikes to get a feel for what suits your behind best. Be forewarned, however, that most seats take some getting used to, especially if you're a novice cyclist. Since most seats are designed for men's hindquarters, women often have a harder job finding one to fit.

The Life You Save May Be Your Own

A helmet can help prevent serious injuries to your head, on road or trail. The British Columbia Medical Association (BCMA) reports that "wearing a bicycle helmet reduces the risk of head injury by 85% and brain injury by 88%" and that "most deaths from bicycle head injuries could be prevented by wearing approved bicycle helmets."(*The Province,* April 21,1991) Children without helmets are especially at risk. The BCMA continues to lobby for mandatory helmet use. When buying a helmet look for ANSI, Snell, or CSA certification. Make sure you get one in a size and style that fits you, and remember to fasten the strap; otherwise it'll abandon you when you need it most.

If you plan to cycle at night, get a light. You might not need a light to see your way, but it will allow others to see you coming. In Vancouver and on the highway, it's mandatory. To avoid consigning dead batteries to landfills, buy a unit with a rechargeable battery or a generator. Generator-powered lights make pedalling a little harder and go out when you stop, whereas a battery with charger costs more to buy and needs periodic recharging. High-intensity and dual-lamp halogen sets are available for more illumination. Reflectors, a taillight, and a reflective vest will also help improve visibility.

A bell is another accessory that is required by law in some cities, such as Vancouver (since 1896).

Using an eyeglass-mounted rearview mirror was like peering into a crystal ball at first, but now I find it's invaluable for keeping track of developments to the rear while remaining focused on happenings ahead. (Always confirm by looking over your shoulder before turning left). Helmet and handlebar mounting models are also available.

Yes, You Can Take It With You

Handlebar, frame, and seat bags can be used to carry a few tools, a snack, or a guidebook. For more capacity, use a fanny pack, a day pack (a large pack is unwieldy and unstable) or panniers. Better quality panniers are generally easier to install and remove than cheap ones, will adjust to keep the load from flopping about, and will last longer, as well. Make sure they don't interfere with your feet. For less demanding trail riding, you can use panniers, but tighten the compression straps. On trickier trails, a fanny pack or a day pack is a better choice. As tandems don't have the luggage space of two single bikes, a trailer may be necessary. Handlebar baskets, although less popular than they once were, are still useful for trips to the market and casual riding. Heavy loads on the handlebars may cause instability at high speed, however.

What Would We Do Without Them? • There are several other accessories you will want to acquire. A water bottle (or two) is virtually a must. Keeping track of speed and distance travelled is easily handled by a cyclecomputer (but be sure to calibrate it). Many have additional features. Handlebar attachments are available to give you more hand positions on an ATB or a better aerodynamic posture on a road bike. A kickstand makes parking easier, but adds weight and can rattle loose. Many cyclists swear by toeclips or, increasingly, by clipless pedal and shoe combinations because they keep the feet in contact with the pedals for more efficient pedalling, on the upstroke as well as the downstroke. Since they take getting used to, practice in a safe area.

Lock It Or Lose It • *Nearly 50% of Vancouver cyclists have lost one or more bikes to theft.*

If you plan to leave your bike unattended even for a few minutes in an urban or suburban area, get a lock. Though no locking system will stop a determined

NEXT PAGE: Gravel dykes offer some of the Lower Mainland's best recreational cycling.

thief, any lock will discourage impulse theft. A high quality U-lock is great for attaching your bike's frame and one or both wheels to bike racks or parking meters, etc. but a sturdy cable or chain is needed to secure your pride and joy to larger objects, such as lamp poles. Avoid cheap combination locks, however. Identification decals and engraved markings can also deter theft and help police return recovered bikes.

Sadly, your bike is only truly safe when you're with it. Even if it is locked, quick-release parts and pumps remain especially vulnerable, and sometimes thieves will even take pedals and handlebars.

Keeping It Roadworthy

Learn how to maintain and repair your bike. *At the very least, know how to replace a punctured tire tube.* Take a continuing education course or get a book from the library or bookstore. Even if you prefer to leave routine jobs to your favourite bike mechanic, it's invaluable to know how to make emergency repairs yourself. Also, you'll notice when your bike needs attention, and you'll be able to help your friends with their bikes.

At least monthly, and before longer trips and off-road trips, check for loose nuts and bolts, loose bearings, frayed cables, rust, tire damage, worn brakes (before they gouge your rims!), etc.

The chain needs periodic cleaning and lubrication: a thin oil or even a paraffin wax treatment for dry or dusty riding and a thicker oil (e.g., automotive oils, motorcycle chain lube) for better staying power when the chain gets wet. Clean the derailleurs and oil the freewheel bearings every once in a while as well. Bearings on the axles, crankset, headset, and pedals should be serviced at least twice a year and perhaps more often (except special lifetime "sealed" units, which need eventual replacing).

If you've got a classy bike, clean (and periodically wax) your frame to protect the paint. Try using a stiff brush (similar to a broom head) and warm, soapy water (trying not to get the bearings wet). Then rinse it clean and finish with a soft cloth.

Winter maintenance is the about the same as for the other seasons, only much more often. Ditto if you regularly ride through a lot of mud and water. A chain can need re-oiling after just one trip. It's also amazing how quickly bottom brackets can go bad. Wipe the muck and grit off your rims and brake shoes to make them last a little longer.

Mechanical First Aid • What should you put into a toolkit? For short trips, you might not bother taking one. For extensive trips away from assistance, you'll want to take spares of almost everything and the tools to replace them. As a compromise for a day trip, consider taking a spare tube and/or tire patches (e.g., the "self-vulcanizing" variety with the orange fringes) and glue (check that it hasn't dried), a pump, a pair of tire lifters, some oil, a small adjustable wrench, and a combination screwdriver and allen wrench tool that fits the bolts and screws on your particular bicycle. If you add a pair of locking pliers, a spoke tool and spare spokes, a chain repair tool, and a few selected spare screws, nuts, and washers, you'll be able to handle most common mechanical emergencies.

If you plan to do most of your own maintenance and repairs, stock your home tool chest with good quality tools — bottom bracket wrenches, freewheel and crank extractors, cone wrenches, etc. or find a friend who will lend them out.

The Well-Dressed Cyclist

Cyclists spending many hours per day in the saddle will often purchase special wool or lycra cycling tights and shorts with soft chamois-lined crotches to reduce chafing. Wash them frequently and carefully. Racers wear jerseys of nylon to cover their upper halves. Many casual riders just wear whatever. Tight jeans are not a good idea, though, especially if it rains. Their thick seams can also cause painful chafing for some riders. If you have loose pant legs, fasten the right one out of reach of the chain, using a metal clip or an elastic band. While you're down there, also tuck in your laces if they dangle.

You can protect your eyes from insects, dust, and overhanging branches with glasses, sunglasses, or goggles. For your feet, special cycling socks are available, incorporating high-tech, moisture-wicking fibres or boasting Kevlar reinforcement. Many riders just wear cotton sports socks and runners for dry-weather cycling.

Shorts and a T-shirt, UV-blocking sunglasses, and a few dabs of suntan lotion will see you comfortably through a sunny summer day trip, but take a lightweight shell jacket along if you're likely to be out past sunset, when it can cool down quickly, especially towards spring and fall. Also consider that cycling coaches and doctors recommend protecting the knee joints with long pants or tights whenever the temperature falls below 16° C (60° F).

Neither Rain Nor Sleet Nor Snow . . .

Especially on chilly days, rain gear can be invaluable if the heavens let loose. Cycling ponchos and raincoats are available from some stores but many cyclists use hiking-style rain jackets. Though clothing made of Goretex or other vapour-permeable materials will keep you slightly drier than rubber or vinyl garments, closable vents are even more important. Since standard rain pants, even those of breathable fabric, are noisy and sweaty on a bicycle, many cyclists don't bother with them except under the worst of conditions or on longer trips. Instead, you might be able to find spats (strap-on, waterproof front-of-the-leg covers); you can also get cycling pants with a waterproof front and a lycra back. If you wear glasses, try a beaked cap under your helmet to help maintain your vision when it's raining or sleeting. Choose eye-arresting colours to make yourself more visible to motorists.

NEXT PAGE: Cycling is a year-round activity.

In winter, dress in layers, as cross-country skiers do. Long underpants, undershirts, and socks, made of polypropylene, wool, or silk, will help wick perspiration away from your skin. Other layers provide insulation and wind/rain protection. Like a skier, be prepared to don more clothing if it gets colder or you stop for a rest or a breakdown.

Cycling gloves (usually fingerless) are used by many cyclists to cushion their hands against road shock and provide some protection in case of misadventure. When it's really cold out, you might try cross-country ski gloves, work gloves, or even downhill ski mitts. Make sure you still have a firm grip on the handlebars and can operate the brakes and gear shifters properly. Cold rain is the hardest to beat; warmth depends both on waterproof gloves and on stopping water from coming in at the cuffs. Experiment till you find the best solution for you.

Surprisingly, cold feet can be a real problem for cyclists; the movements of walking are much more effective for keeping them warm. Waterproof and possibly insulated shoe covers (of coated nylon, Goretex, neoprene, etc.) will help keep your feet dry and toasty. Even if you use water-resistant shoes, you'll still benefit from rainpants or gaiters to keep the rain from trickling down your socks. Some cyclists are successful with tight-fitting rubber boots, or sailing boots with a drawstring; for occasional and temporary use others employ plastic bags (e.g., bread bags) over their feet, inside their shoes, sealed at the top with duct tape or elastic bands.

To keep your face warm on those rare arctic days when water pipes are bursting, wear a balaclava and possibly goggles. A scarf or a high collar helps keep the chills off your neck. Use petroleum jelly or lip balm to prevent your lips and other sensitive facial skin from freeze-drying and cracking.

What You Can't See . . .

In the "intangibles" category, you might want to contemplate insurance: theft, vandalism, or own-damage insurance (if not included in your home-owner's or tenant's policy), medical insurance (if you ride outside of Canada), and third-party liability insurance (in case someone sues you for injury to person or property).

In the beginning, people straddled pedal-less hobby horses; later they rode penny-farthings. As the years went by, the bicycle evolved into a solid, heavy workhorse, equipped with balloon tires and coaster brake. People cycled on whatever roads and tracks were available. Roads improved. Lighter, faster three-speeds ("English racers") became popular in the '60s. With the development of fragile featherweight multi-speed bicycles ("10-speeds"), riders became fussier and largely abandoned the rougher routes.

Marin County, California, saw the rebirth of the sturdy bike in the late 1970s, enhanced with lightweight exotic alloys and equipped with high-performance components. At first each bike was custom-built but by 1982 the first production bikes (Specialized Stumpjumpers) were on the market. Less than a decade later, U.S. sales of fat-tire bikes topped those for road bikes.

ORGANIZATIONS TO CONTACT

For more information on recreational or competitive cycling, contact the following groups.

OUTDOOR RECREATION COUNCIL OF BC (ORC)
#334, 1367 W Broadway
Vancouver, BC, V6H 4A9
(737-3058)
• an umbrella organization of recreational organizations (FMCBC and BABC are members) that liaises with various government agencies and departments and the private sector, promotes recreational activities, and coordinates symposia on issues such as rails-to-trails and mountain biking

BICYCLING ASSOCIATION OF BRITISH COLUMBIA (BABC)
#332, 1367 West Broadway
Vancouver, BC, V6H 4A9
(recorded msg. hotline: 731-RIDE, real people: 737-3034)
(may be moving to new bicycle track on Barnet Hwy)
• the provincial umbrella group for all sanctioned road, track, and off-road racing activity; also covers recreation, education, transportation, and advocacy issues

Some Greater Vancouver Cycling Clubs

CROSS CANADA CYCLE TOUR SOCIETY
#315, 1367 W Broadway
Vancouver, BC, V6H 4A9
(737-3112)   *(may be moving)*
• a group of (mostly) seniors that organizes frequent recreational trips, including many camping trips, and longer tours across Canada and overseas ($20/yr, families $30)

VANCOUVER BICYCLE CLUB
Box 2235 Main PO
Vancouver, BC, V6B 3W2
-day trips and longer tours for individuals and families, also social events
($25/yr, families $30)

RICHMOND BICYCLE CLUB
c/o Frank Bernstein, 273-3372
• recreational rides Tuesday evening from early April, and twice-monthly on
Sundays from May until late September; also social events, overnighters, Polar
Bear ride, a 10-day trip, etc. ($18/yr, fam. $28, students $13)

FEDERATION OF MOUNTAIN CLUBS OF BC (FMCBC)
#336, 1367 W Broadway
Vancouver, BC, V6H 4A9
(737-3053)   *(planning a move; please consult your phone book)*
• the provincial umbrella organization for clubs involved in hiking, mountain-
eering, backpacking, etc.

FMCBC member clubs with a recreational cycling component
(membership typ. $18-$25/yr):

KLISTER OUTDOOR KLUB
c/o FMCBC
OUTSETTERS CLUB
PO Box 33903, Station D
Vancouver, BC, V6J 4L7

Cycling for the Physically Challenged
There are many bicycling enthusiasts in the Lower Mainland who have a great
time cycling in spite of what some people might consider to be prohibitive
handicaps. In addition to recreational riding, there are opportunities to compete
provincially, nationally, and internationally (the highlight is the Paralympics).

For more information, or if you would like to volunteer your help, please contact these associations:

AMPUTEE SPORTS ASSOCIATION OF BC
#322, 1367 W Broadway
Vancouver, BC, V6H 4A9
(Madeleine Anderson, 251-7444)

BLIND SPORTS AND RECREATION ASSOCIATION OF BC
#317, 1367 W. Broadway
Vancouver, BC, V6H 4A9
(Jane Blaine, 325-8638)

CEREBRAL PALSY SPORTS ASSOCIATION OF BC
#300, 8356 120th St
Surrey, BC, V3W 3N4
(Terrie Moore, 599-5240)

DEAF SPORTS ASSOCIATION OF BC
#218, 1367 W. Broadway
Vancouver, BC, V6H 4A9
(call BC Tel's TDD number, 681-2913, and ask operator for 738-7122)

GETTING WHERE YOU'RE GOING

You've got several choices in getting to the start of a route, among them: use your car or truck, carry your bike on public transit (see below), take transit there and rent a bike, or ride your bike from home.

Let's consider that last option in more detail. Many a cycling trip has been nipped in the bud because cyclists became discouraged during the planning stages, wondering how to deal with obstacles along the route. This reference section will shed some light on those mysteries. (For more information, consult the BABC/VBC map showing the cyclability of Vancouver streets, and the (planned) GVRD regional map showing designated routes.)

Getting there can be half the fun or a dreadful experience; it depends on your choice of route, your skill, and your attitude. The secondary roads (or tertiary ones) will generally be the most interesting and relaxing, while the highways and arterials will be faster but busier. Here are some general tips to use in conjunction with a regular road map (see also the chapter on **Advocacy**).

A bicycle courier takes to the street in Vancouver's Gastown.

Vancouver to New Westminster

Vancouver streets are largely laid out on a grid with most of the traffic on the arterials. Secondary roads are quieter and are often through-roads, but alignment can be poor and unsigned intersections abound. They can take you most places in the city, except downtown, though you still have to cross those arterials. The less pleasant arterials include 1st Ave from Boundary Rd to Clark St; Clark St/ Knight St, esp. from 12th Ave to Knight St Bridge and beyond; Prior/Venables from Main St to Commercial Dr.; Grandview Hwy/12th Ave/Kitsilano Diversion/10th Ave, from Nanaimo St to Alma St; Oak St from King Edward Ave south, worse closer to Oak St bridge; Marine Way/SE Marine Drive, esp. from Boundary to Knight St; much of S Granville St; and notably Kingsway during the morning rush hour. Most of Vancouver is upland, descending towards the north and south sides.

Further east, Burnaby and New Westminster streets are also laid out according to a grid, though perhaps 20 % is at 45 degrees to the rest. Secondary streets are better over shorter distances. North-south travel in particular is likely to be hindered by steeper slopes and Hwy 1. Among the less enjoyable roads are North Rd/E Columbia St from Lougheed Hwy to 8th Ave and esp. from Brunette Ave to downtown New West; Brunette Ave from Lougheed Hwy; McBride Blvd from Pattullo Bridge to 10th Ave; 10th Ave between McBride Blvd and 12th St; Canada Way from 10th Ave to Boundary Rd, esp. between Imperial Ave and Kensington Ave; Stewardson Way/North Arm Drive from 8th St to Marine Way; Boundary Rd south of Hwy 1; Rumble St east of Royal Oak Ave.

The North Shore

On the North Shore, you're going to encounter hills inland. Marine Dr. and the Upper Levels Hwy/Hwy 1/99 provide the only long-haul east-west connections. East of the Second Narrows, through-roads are limited to Mount Seymour Parkway and Dollarton Hwy and a few north-south links. From the centre of West Vancouver to the Second Narrows Bridge and south of Hwy 1 and a section across Hwy 1 from the City of North Vancouver the roads are mostly laid out to follow the standard grid, giving many options. If you want to know where the winding roads lead, you'll need a map. Residential sprawl predominates.

Richmond and Delta

Richmond is flat. In urban areas, traffic is heavily concentrated on the (mostly four-lane) gridlike arterials; the secondary roads are hit-or-miss without a map. Rural roads are mostly quite pleasant, though. Only Westminster Hwy and River Rd allow cyclists to travel continuously through eastern Richmond.

Most of Delta is also flat, except for the climbs into the Tsawwassen and North Delta uplands. Urban concentrations are in N Delta, Tsawwassen, and Ladner; excepting an industrial zone, the rest is fairly rural.

Connections across the Fraser River are limited (see below); the lack of full-time provision for cyclists to cross at the George Massey Tunnel—or anytime at the Port Mann Bridge—makes for lengthy detours, added expense, or cancelled cycling trips. Another problem is the lack of a convenient link from Delta to S Surrey: cyclists are not permitted to follow the direct, hill-free paths taken by Hwy 91 and Hwy 99 but must detour via the uplands in order to reach King George Hwy.

Bridges and Ferries: a guide to the where's and how's of crossing water

Watch for bumpy expansion joints and for dips at the ends of bridge sidewalks. When sharing narrow sidewalks, yield the right-of-way to pedestrians and to cyclists coming downhill towards you; ring your bell or call out, especially if approaching from behind. When sharing roadways with motorists, use extra care when crossing

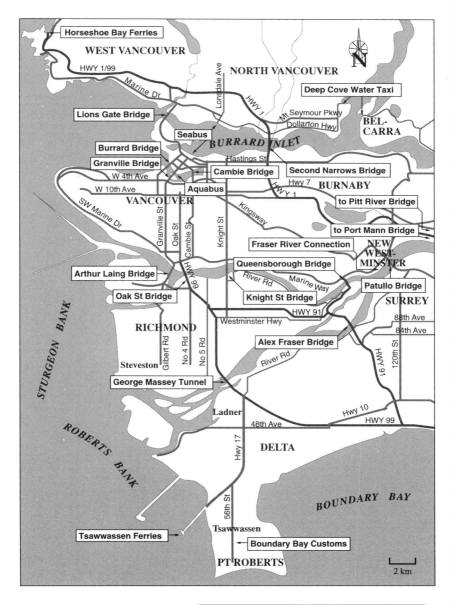

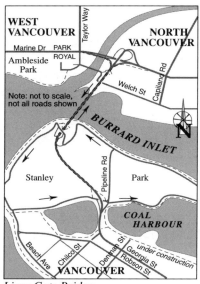

Lions Gate Bridge.

on ramps and exits—consider planning your route to use the last on ramp and the first exit—and watch for vehicles cutting right-hand curves.

Burrard Inlet and Indian Arm •
(least stressful way to cross Burrard Inlet is on the Seabus)

• *Lions Gate (First Narrows) Bridge*
(Vancouver to West Vancouver; Hwy 99/Hwy 1A)

Use one-directional sidewalks. Not for the faint of heart: sidewalks are narrow, bumpy, and close to traffic. Signage is poor. At the N end, the descent to the underpass and Welch St is steep. If you use the underpass at the S end of the bridge, beware the low clearance, blind corner, and dropoff. Through Stanley Pk use the sidewalk along the smelly, noisy highway or else take quieter Pipeline Rd or Park Dr. instead.

• *Seabus* (Vancouver to North Vancouver; 601 W Cordova between Granville St and Seymour St on S side; Lonsdale Quay, W along Esplanade from Lonsdale Ave, or from foot of Chesterfield Ave on N side) Off-peak hours only (every 15-30 min, approx. Mon-Fri 9:30 am-3 pm and 6:30 pm-12:30 am, Sat 6:45 am-12:30 am, Sun/Hol 8:45 am-11 pm), single fare ($1.35). Max. 6 bikes per trip. Use elevator just E of escalators on Van. side. Attendant will open door to bypass turnstile. Use rear door of ferry. Approx. 12 min. crossing on *Burrard Beaver* and *Burrard Otter*.

• *Second Narrows Bridge* (Vancouver to North Vancouver; Hwy 1) (note: S approach being rebuilt in 1991-2)

On both sidewalks (slightly wider than on Lions Gate Bridge, and somewhat smoother). Not properly signposted. From the Vancouver side, reach the E sidewalk by crossing over Hwy 1 at Triumph St, Hastings St, or at Adanac St or Charles St. Coming off

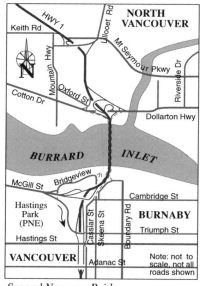

Second Narrows Bridge.

the E sidewalk in N Vancouver, you are obligated to go E on Main St/Dollarton Hwy; to go W or N, look for a chance to leave the sidewalk and do a U-turn, or continue E and go N on Riverside Dr. Getting onto the W sidewalk from North Vancouver is easiest at the corner of Cotton Dr./Main St and Mountain Hwy. Leaving the W sidewalk is via a bumpy, gravel-strewn two-hairpin ramp; then if you're headed E, it's a narrow, uphill tunnel on Skeena St, or a detour via Bridgeway St.

• *Deep Cove Water Taxi* (Deep Cope to Belcarra)

Departs from the main dock at Deep Cove and the dock at the Belcarra Regional Park Picnic Area. Also goes to other places. $5/bike, minimum charge $15. Call ahead: 929-3011.

False Creek • (least stressful crossing is by Aquabus)

• *Burrard St Bridge* One-directional on sidewalks. SW bound, access at N end is good, then take ramp down to road at S end of bridge. If continuing S on Burrard St, use extreme caution crossing two lanes of traffic (or use pedestrian light) and watch for following cyclists. NW bound, access at S end is good, then use extra care at N end if continuing on Burrard St, or if joining Pacific St E bound beyond the alley.

• *Granville St Bridge* (Hwy 99)

On road. Busy and fast.

• *Aquabus*

Ferry docks behind Arts Club Theatre (Granville Is.), False Creek Yacht Club (under N end of Granville Bridge), and foot of Hornby St; 7:30 am-9 pm, $1.25, can only take a few bikes at the time. Information: 874-9930

• *Cambie St Bridge*

On road. Busy and fast.

FRASER RIVER

• *Arthur Laing Bridge* (Vancouver to Sea Island/Airport, Richmond)

On road. Busy and fast. Paved shoulders most of the way.

• *Oak St Bridge* (Vancouver to Richmond; Hwy 99)

On sidewalks only. S bound there is no ramp onto the sidewalk at the Vancouver end, and neither ramps nor crosswalk to facilitate continuing on past the first exit to No. 4 Rd. From Sea Island Way N bound, there's a big loop to cycle or bypass, then the only exit is

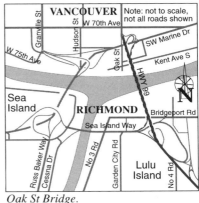

Oak St Bridge.

SW Marine Drive E bound. (Hey, Oak St isn't much fun to cycle anyway.) To go W, circle around under the bridge on Shaughnessy St and Kent Ave N to the traffic light at Oak St and SW Marine Dr.

• *Knight St Bridge* (Vancouver to Richmond and Mitchell Island)

Poorly located signs tell you to use the sidewalks, but most cyclists use the paved shoulders instead. Warning: they collect outstanding quantities of junk. Busy and fast. S bound it can be tricky getting to the second (E bound) exit at Bridgeport Rd. Note that Knight St is unpleasant to cycle at most times of the day.

• *George Massey Tunnel* (Richmond to Delta; Hwy 99)

No cycling permitted. Traditionally, a free, seasonal passenger van/bicycle trailer service carries cyclists through the tunnel. Typically it runs on the last two weekends of May, daily from June to the end of August, and on September weekends, with S bound trips at 8 am, 11 am, 3 pm, and 7 pm, and N bound ones departing half an hour later, though the schedule may vary. Extra trips are made in case of excess demand. Pickup points are at Rice Mill Rd where it crosses Hwy 99 (access from No. 5 Rd in S Richmond) and on the northwest side of the Hwy 99 Hwy 17/62B St interchange in Delta. Call the Ministry of Transportation at 660-8300 to confirm times of operation. If the service is not operating, detour via Alex Fraser Bridge, summon a taxi, or try hitchhiking at safe locations near freeway access points.

• *Queensborough & Alex Fraser Bridges* (New Westminster to Richmond, Annacis Island, and Delta; Hwy 91/91A)

On sidewalks, paths, and secondary roads; cycling is not permitted on Hwy 91/91A itself. Depending on starting point and destination, expect to find pedestrian overpass and underpasses, spiral ramp, slippery steel surfaces, flooded sections, and blind corners (latter two threats near jct. of Nordel Way and Hwy 91). Watch out for cable anchors and sign standards on the Alex Fraser Bridge. Officially, you're expected to use the SE sidewalk along Nordel Way, coming or going. Access to S Surrey is poor.

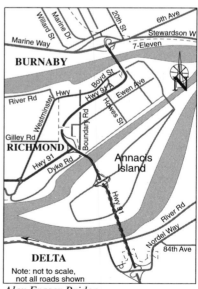

Alex Fraser Bridge.

• *Fraser River Connection* (from immediately east of New Westminster Quay to Fort Langley and return)

The Native, a 100-passenger, 28 m diesel-powered paddlewheeler takes scheduled sightseeing trips along the Fraser River (and elsewhere); May-Oct only, boarding at 9:30 am, reaching Fort Langley at 12:30 pm, with departure at 2:30 pm and finish at 4 pm; $25 return or $20 one way; call ahead to book: 525-4465

• *Pattullo Bridge* (New Westminster to Surrey; Hwy 1A/99A)

Use sidewalk (only one, on S side). Access to the N end is (roughly in order of increasing traffic speed) via Agnes St, Dufferin St, and a path; Royal Avenue; Columbia St; or McBride Blvd. On reaching the Surrey side, there's a bit of a detour via 110th Ave and 128th St if you want to regain Hwy 1A/99A. Heading W on Hwy 1A/99A also involves a detour, underneath the bridge, or via 128th St and 110th Ave (note: there are other access roads too). At the New West end, the official route is the path up to Wellington St and Dufferin St; otherwise, you could sneak down the sidewalk to Columbia St.

• *Port Mann Bridge* (Coquitlam to Surrey; Hwy 1)

No cyclists or pedestrians; open to vehicles capable of 60 km/h only.

PITT RIVER

• *Pitt River Bridge* (Coquitlam to Pitt Meadows; Hwy 7/Lougheed Hwy)

On road. Twin swing bridges. W bound bridge has 1 m paved shoulder and sidewalk. E bound bridge has neither.

BC Ferries • Pay at a vehicular toll booth (optionally with the pedestrians). Fares given below are 1991, one way. For a recorded schedule of Mainland Van. Island routes, call 685-1021; for other routes or information (7 am-10 pm daily) it's 669-1211.

• *Tsawwassen Ferry* (Hwy 17; access from Hwy 10, River Rd, or Hwy 99 summer tunnel shuttle; Delta)

• to Swartz Bay (Victoria) (about 12 trips/day each way, 20 in summer): $5.50 + $2.50 for bike

• to Nanaimo (4 trips, 8 in summer): as above

• to Southern Gulf Islands (2-3 trips, 3-4 in summer): $4.50 + $2.50; or ask for a *through fare* with a transfer to the next avail. ferry at Swartz Bay (3-4 trips, 5-6 in summer): $5.50 + $2.50

• *Horseshoe Bay Ferry* (Hwy 1, or Marine Dr-Nelson Ave-Chatham-Royal-Bay St, W Vancouver)

• to Nanaimo (8 trips): $5.50 + $2.50

• to Sunshine Coast (8-9 trips): $5.50 + $2.50 (return)

• to Bowen Island (15 trips): $3.50 + $1.50 (return)

Border Crossings

Southbound cyclists must report to U.S. customs, northbound cyclists to Canadian customs. Go to the regular booths. Most cyclists bypass the traffic lineup and most motorists will tolerate this. Carry proof of citizenship or you might be refused entry to the USA. If your bike looks new, Canada customs may charge you duty on your return! Avoid this by getting a green Y-38 card for your bike (and items such as expensive cameras, etc.) from customs prior to leaving the country. To limit the spread of disease, travellers are forbidden to carry certain agricultural products across the border. Also consider extra health insurance, especially for extended trips.

PORT HOURS AND APPROACH
• **Boundary Bay**

    24 hr; 56th St, off Hwy 17; Delta

Highways

Bikes are permitted on most BC highways, except freeways. Although riding next to fast, dense traffic isn't much fun, and other options often exist, there are times you'll need or want to do so. *Use extreme caution when crossing onramps and exits.* Here is a guide to access on Greater Vancouver highways otherwise closed to cyclists (current as of fall 1991):

• *Hwy 1:* closed to cycling *except for* the shoulders of the North Shore's Upper Levels Hwy, W of Capilano Rd only

• *Hwy 91/91A:* closed to cycling *except for* sidewalks/bike paths—see Alex Fraser Bridge

• *Hwy 99:* closed to cycling *except for*

• through Vancouver to Upper Levels Hwy in North Vancouver—see Oak St and Lions Gate bridges

• shoulders of Upper Levels Highway—see Hwy 1

• north of Horseshoe Bay

Taking Your Bike out of Town on Public Transit

Here is a guide to carriers, destinations, {sample 1991 one way fares from Vancouver}, [bike surcharge], packaging required and comments, Vancouver address, and phone number (check local phone books or phone for others). Note that most of these carriers will not reserve space (packing bikes last), require you to travel with your bike, load/unload bikes only at depots, and will not take responsibility for damage.

• **BC Rail**: N. Vancouver, Squamish, Whistler {$13.50}, Pemberton, D'Arcy, Lillooet (all once per day [$6.50]), 100 Mile House, Williams Lake, Prince George (all 3 x per week [$13.00]; pkg not req'd, reservations taken for passengers only; 1311 W 1st St (at Pemberton Ave), North Vancouver, recorded info: 631-3501, reservations & info: 631-3500

• **BC Transit**: doesn't presently take bikes, except on Seabus (unless you can fold them up and bag them or disguise them as something else), but may in the future (see Advocacy)

• **Cascade Charter Service Ltd**: Vancouver, Maple Ridge, Mission {$5.95}, Langley, Abbotsford, Chilliwack {$8.20} [all free]; box, bag, or wrap; downtown depot at 150 Dunsmuir St, 662-7953

• **Greyhound Lines of Canada Ltd**: Vancouver, many other places in Fraser Valley, BC, and across Canada and USA (e.g., Chilliwack {$9.90} [$13.45+GST], Whistler {no service} [$9.25+GST]); box bike and send it ahead via Greyhound Courier Express, 455 Industrial Ave (door-to-door service available at higher cost in some locations) 681-3526; passengers depart from 150 Dunsmuir St, 662-3222

• **Maverick Coach Lines**:: Vancouver, Vancouver Island (via Nanaimo), Squamish, Whistler {$12.85}, Pemberton, Sunshine Coast (Sechelt {$14.40}) [all $10]; box recommended; downtown depot at 150 Dunsmuir St, 662-8051

• **Pacific Coach Lines**: Vancouver, Victoria {$19.70} [$5.35]; pkg not req'd; downtown depot at 150 Dunsmuir St, 662-8074

• **Perimeter Transportation Ltd**: Vancouver, Int'l Airport {$8.25}, Whistler (winter and summer) {$26.75} [free]; box, phone ahead to confirm; several pickup points, airport info: 273-9023, Whistler info: 261-2299

• **Taxis**: Many taxi companies will take bicycles, too. By no means bargain transportation, they can nevertheless help out when you have a breakdown or injury, or want to avoid an obstacle. Sample rates: through the George Massey Tunnel (Hwy 99), about $10; from downtown Vancouver to Ladner or Horseshoe Bay, $30–35.

ADVOCACY: WORKING FOR BETTER ACCESS AND SAFER CYCLING

There are many people in Greater Vancouver who would cycle more often, for both recreation and transportation, were it not for safety concerns. Would-be commuter cyclists are also deterred by a lack of secure parking facilities. These deficiencies need to be addressed by educating cyclists and motorists on successful coexistence, and, equally importantly, by treating cycling as an integral component in transportation planning.

Although designated bike routes and major facilities have a place in making cycling safer and more attractive, frequently it's smaller touches such as building wider curb lanes, permitting cyclists to bypass traffic diverters, providing even a 1.5 m wide paved shoulder along highways, or installing showers in the work place that make the difference between a reluctant cyclist and one who feels welcome.

If you find your cycling is hampered by inadequate maintenance or poor design, why not do something about it? After all, cycling advocacy has a rich tradition dating back to the late 1800s, even predating the automobile.

Cycling advocates—ordinary people like you and me.

Maintenance problems, such as potholes or debris, can often be resolved with a call to the city/municipal works yard, usually found in the phone book under "engineering" for that jurisdiction (in Vancouver, it's 327-8121). For provincial highways, look in the blue pages for the appropriate private contractor for each district.

Concerns involving design or policy changes, or unresolved maintenance problems, should be brought to the attention of engineering and planning staff, or elected politicians. Letters and phone calls not only address the specific problem but also encourage the consideration of cyclists' needs in general. Face-to-face meetings will be even more effective. Strengthen the effect of your letters by sending copies to advocacy groups such as Vancouver's Bicycle Advisory Committee and the Bicycling Association of BC.

The State Of The Art

The last few years, and mid-to-late 1991 in particular, have seen an incredible surge in bicycle-related planning activity in Greater Vancouver. The following is a synopsis of what exists or is in progress, as interpreted from conversations with members of planning and engineering staffs.

Cities and Districts • You may need to talk to the recreation, planning, traffic, or engineering departments. For reports and plans, try the city/municipal clerk's office. For official political recognition of your concerns or congratulations, address your letter to "Mayor and Council."

Water breaks provide welcome relief in hilly North Burnaby

BURNABY Bike lanes partially improve access to the SFU campus on Burnaby Mountain and there is a halfway-to-adequate bicycle bypass where Kensington Ave meets Lougheed Hwy. Undesignated paved shoulders along much of Barnet Hwy, Lougheed Hwy, and Marine Way assist east-west commuter travel.

Recreational cycling occurs in Central Park; cyclist use of Burnaby's many other trails (e.g., on Burnaby Mountain) is not presently condoned by the municipality. A planned Urban Trail System comprises three each north-south and east-west routes (including the 7-Eleven Trail), with partial separation of pedestrians and cyclists, to be constructed one every two years. The first section of new trail (across southwest Burnaby Mountain) is expected to open in spring of 1992.

Also, developers are being encouraged to include bicycle storage and parking, and new roads are being constructed with wider curb lanes.

DELTA   Several seashore dykes are informally open to cyclists. The Corporation of Delta Parks and Recreation Master Plan (Mar. 1989) includes a goal to "develop a pedestrian and bicycle trail system that will provide access to the ocean and the river, [and] connect the three urban areas . . . ." River Road/62B St has a designated bicycle/pedestrian lane presently suitable for westbound cycling only. Several roads have paved shoulders, including Hwy 17 (wide),

Ladner Harbour: the fishing fleet at rest.

Hwy 10 (narrow), and Boundary Bay Road. There is a proposal to include in several area plans a recommendation that cycling routes be established, probably to be implemented incrementally as roads are upgraded.

NEW WESTMINSTER   There are no current cycling-related plans. Existing narrow rights-of-way make road widening difficult; few new roads are laid.

NORTH VANCOUVER CITY & DISTRICT   There is a pair of cycling lanes along Mt Seymour Parkway, but there is room for improvement elsewhere, too. The North Shore Transportation Study of the late '80s addressed automobile usage and dangerous goods movement, but not cycling. This oversight is now about to be corrected by the North Shore Bicycle Routes Committee, struck in late 1991. Including district and city representatives from parks and traffic departments, it hopes to address the needs of both recreational and commuter cyclists. A preliminary plan is expected for late 1992/early 1993, with implementation to take several years.

RICHMOND   Richmond has well-signed bike lanes that follow Granville and Railway Avenues.There were built around 1980 after the release of the 1978 Richmond Bicycle Plan. There are paved shoulders on several roads, including Grant McConachie Way, and parts of Garden City Rd and Westminster Hwy. The longest stretch of recreational dyke trail follows the shoreline from the Moray Channel Bridge to Steveston; other lengths of cycling/pedestrian path are distributed along much of Richmond's other shorelines and inland. Signage to link them via regular roads is planned for 1992. Also expected is the formation of a new bicycle committee; it would revise the 1978 plan using the results of an upcoming cyclist survey. Recreation, engineering, and planning departments are working together to develop a comprehensive network of cycling routes and trails over the next few years, under the informal banner of "Circumcycling Richmond."

UNIVERSITY OF BRITISH COLUMBIA (UBC)   There are narrow paved bike paths (one side only) along NW Marine Drive (shared with pedestrians), Chancellor Blvd (shared), University Blvd, and W 16th Ave, with paved shoulders along SW Marine Drive most of the way to Granville St. A network of dirt and gravel bicycle-accessible trails is located in the surrounding Pacific Spirit Regional Park (see Route V14). On the campus itself, cyclists are not restricted to designated areas but are free to mingle with the throngs of pedestrians on service roads, or with the cars on open roads. Bike racks have been placed in many locations. Improvements are being sought by members of the Student Environment Centre.

VANCOUVER   The city's oldest and busiest recreational cycling route is on the Stanley Park Seawall. Several Stanley Park trails are also open to cycling. The largely recreational Seaside Route (around False Creek and west to Spanish Banks) also serves some utilitarian needs, mostly via its "bypass" sections. Routes are in progress along the Fraser River (Fraserlands, Elliot to Kerr) and Burrard Inlet (Canada Harbour Place to Stanley Park).

The responsibility for taking cyclists into account is distributed throughout engineering, parks, and other departments. Though this approach has the advantage of integrating cycling into mainstream thought, many cyclists feel that the restoration of the bicycle coordinator position is crucial. The basis of city bicycle standards is formed by the 1988 *Vancouver Comprehensive Bicycle Plan* (VCBP), supplemented by subsequent reports and bylaws. The VCBP makes recommendations in the fields of engineering, education, enforcement, and encouragement. Of these, two-thirds are considered completed and ongoing, and the rest (largely encouragement) are "in progress," though a few are on hold.

The preferred alternative for improving bicycle safety in the city is enhanced integration on local streets, using a network of bicycle routes on quieter roads. It will likely be implemented beginning in late 1992, based on the work of groups such as the ones below. Bicycle parking standards bylaws have also been enacted.

When the police, school board, parks board, and engineering department have questions related to cycling, they consult the **Bicycle Advisory Committee (BAC)**. This engineering-oriented committee—nine appointees, liaisons from city council and these bodies themselves, and support staff—holds open monthly meetings. Subcommittees are struck to tackle particular issues such as design standards. Contact the BAC c/o City Hall, 453 W 12th Ave, Vancouver, BC V5Y 1V4 or phone the city clerk's office at 873-7275.

The **Vancouver Bikeway Network Group** proposes a city-wide system of bicycle routes (bikeways) on lesser-used streets that run adjacent to arterials. Crossing of perpendicular arterials would be aided by installing cyclist-activated traffic lights, synchronized with those on the adjacent parallel arterial. Contact the Bikeway Network Group through city hall's BAC.

The **Kitsilano Cycling Working Group** of the **Kitsilano Citizens Planning Committee** considered cycling from a neighbourhood perspective to develop the *Kitsilano Bicycle Plan* (Sept. 1991). The plan recommends a series of measures to "promote the safe use of the bicycle by creating an environment which most, if not all, cyclists will find safe, convenient, and comfortable . . . [and] by educating cyclists, motorists, and pedestrians about their rights and responsibilities . . . ." It calls for a "network of 'bicycle friendly streets' in Kitsilano," to comprise Cornwall Ave/Pt Grey Rd, W 8th Ave, W 16th Ave, Arbutus Rail Corridor/Cypress St, Macdonald St, and Waterloo St. Make contact through the BAC or BEST.

WEST VANCOUVER   An old recreational route is marked by signs leading west from Ambleside Park; other signs direct cyclists around on/off ramps on Hwy 1/Hwy 99. The official community plan makes no reference to cycling, but the municipality is considering improvements to facilities (e.g., racks) along the waterfront. Also, parts of Marine Drive are to be widened.

AT A REGIONAL LEVEL

Greater Vancouver Regional District (GVRD). The GVRD has resolved to "reverse transportation priorities so decisions are made to favour walking, cycling, public transit, goods movement and then the automobile." (*Creating Our Future: Steps to a more Livable Region*, 1990) In addition, it proposes to "double the number of bicycle commuters by 1995 through promoting a regional cycling network in cooperation with municipalities, preparing a regional map of commuter and recreational cycling routes, working with B.C. Transit to facilitate multi-modal travel, and encouraging municipalities to adopt development standards that accommodate the needs of cyclists." The first stages of this process have included setting up the Task Force on Cycling, comprising eight mayors and council members as well as a region wide survey of cyclists' needs.

Cycling is permitted in only a few regional parks: Pacific Spirit, Iona Beach, Matsqui Trail, and Seymour Demonstration Forest. Especially with encouragement, the GVRD can be expected to include cycling facilities in future park planning.

Comments and suggestions on policy may be addressed to: Chairperson, GVRD Board of Directors, 4330 Kingsway, Burnaby, BC V5H 4G8 (phone 432-6215). Planners can be contacted directly through Development Services, 432-6375. For parks issues: Chairperson, GVRD Park Committee (same address, 432-6350).

AT A PROVINCIAL LEVEL

BC Parks   There are designated cycling trails in Cypress and Mt Seymour Provincial Parks. Park master plans are periodically opened to public input; however, letters may be written at any time. Address them to: Vancouver District Manager, BC Parks, Box 7000, Maple Ridge, BC, V2X 7G3 (463-3513). Further north, there's a popular cycling trail in Garibaldi Provincial Park; contact the Garibaldi/Sunshine Coast District at Box 220, Brackendale, BC, V0N 1H0 (898-3678/9313). Both districts are in the Lower Mainland Region, with headquarters at 1610 Mt Seymour Road, North Vancouver, BC, V7G 1L3 (929-1291). At a province-wide level, there's the Minister of Environment, Lands and Parks, Parliament Buildings, Victoria, BC, V8V 4R3.

Protesting inadequate design—Bicycle People at the Cassiar Connector.

BC Parks may also assume management of some rails-to-trails routes as abandoned railway rights-of-way are converted into walking/cycling/equestrian trails (see ORC, below).

BC Transit   BC Transit runs several fleets of buses (the largest is in the Greater Vancouver area), the Seabus service across Burrard Inlet, and Skytrain (which operates as a separate arm and is responsible for the bike path along the BC Parkway). The Seabus is open to bicycles during off-peak hours; expanded service may be considered once capacity has been increased by an additional ferry. At least 18 Skytrain and park-and-ride sites have bicycle racks. Lockers, which provide more protection, have been installed on a trial basis (until end of 1992) at Sexsmith (Richmond) and Ladner park-and-rides and at Scott Road Station; rental is on a quarterly basis. If the locker program is successful, it may be expanded to include casual users. Leasing is administered by the BABC (737-3034).

The carrying of bicycles on buses and Skytrain is being contemplated, but involves questions of liability, cost-return, maintenance, access, operator training, etc. Bicycle racks on buses will probably be considered in 1993. Skytrain use may be reassessed once second-generation Mark 2 cars ("Fat Alberts") come into service.

The 7-Eleven Bicycle Route roughly follows the BC Parkway and is largely recreational. It leads from Main Street Station in Vancouver to New Westminster Quay (with a spur to Kingsway at Edmonds St), on paved paths, gravel paths, roads, and sidewalks. Many cyclists consider it a good idea in principle, but feel it could be improved, most notably the on-street routing west of Broadway Station and the road crossings in the Metrotown Central Park area. The best parts are arguably between 22nd St Station and Royal Oak Station. Submit your suggestions for improvements to Skytrain (BC Rapid Transit Co. Ltd, 6800 14th Ave, Burnaby, BC, V3N 4S7, 520-3641), local planners, and/or the addresses in the next paragraph.

Policy is generally set by the Vancouver Regional Transit Commission (BC Transit, 1200 W 73rd Ave, Vancouver, BC, V6P 6M2) with input from and implementation by the planning department (Pura Noriega, Transit Planning, same address). For transit information, call 261-5100; to make commendations or complaints about transit service or staff, call 264-5266. BC Transit is controlled by Minister of Finance and Corporate Relations, Parliament Buildings, Victoria, BC, V8V 1X4.

Ministry of Transportation and Highways (MoTH) The Ministry of Transportation and Highways is developing a new policy regarding cycling, based in part on discussions with BABC representatives. Ministry sources say the new policy will represent a "much more progressive approach." Since it is expected to apply only to new projects and major upgrades, with no provision for automatic improvements to existing highways and bridges, we will likely retain a legacy of the previous minimalist approach for some time to come. Ironically, since this ministry is very "number-driven," cyclists are taken into account only to the extent that they show up in the traffic counts on the presently inadequate facilities.

To suggest improvements to MoTH highways and roads, contact the Senior Traffic Operations Engineer at the appropriate regional office: Howe Sound-Sunshine Coast (987-9311) for areas north of Burrard Inlet, and Lower Mainland (660-8300) for the region from Vancouver to Surrey. If unsuccessful, or to comment on general policy, address your concerns directly to: Minister of Transportation and Highways, Parliament Buildings, Victoria, BC, V8V 1X4.

Advocacy Groups

Non-governmental groups actively promoting cycling or working for improvements to access and facilities include the following:

*BETTER ENVIRONMENTALLY SOUND TRANSPORTATION
(BEST) ASSOCIATION*
PO Box 65803, Station F
Vancouver, BC, V5N 5L1
• encourages greater, more effective, and safer use of bicycles, especially in the Greater Vancouver area, largely through promotional activities and information sharing

BICYCLING ASSOCIATION OF BRITISH COLUMBIA (BABC)
#332, 1367 W Broadway
Vancouver, BC, V6H 4A9
737-3034 (may move to new bicycle track on Barnet Hwy)
• participates in advocacy at provincial and local levels and plans to publish an advocacy manual

EXTREME MOUNTAINBIKE PEOPLE SOCIETY (EMP)
5051 Quebec St
Vancouver, BC, V5W 2N3
327-2547
• develops the sport of mountain biking through negotiations with land managers and cycling industry and through education, trail construction and race organization

RAILS-TO-TRAILS STRATEGY GROUP (not yet named as of this writing)
c/o Outdoor Recreation Council of BC (ORC)
#334, 1367 W Broadway
Vancouver, BC, V6H 4A9
737-3058
• promotes the conversion of abandoned railway rights-of-way to hiking/cycling/equestrian trails

VANCOUVER BICYCLE CLUB
Box 2235 Main PO
Vancouver, BC, V6B 3W2
• becomes involved in recreational advocacy issues

The following groups actively encourage cycling as an alternative to automotive use:

GREEN PARTY OF CANADA
831 Commercial Dr.
Vancouver, BC, V5L 3W6
254-8165

GREENPEACE
1726 Commercial Dr.
Vancouver, BC, V5N 4A3
253-7701

SOCIETY PROMOTING ENVIRONMENTAL CONSERVATION (SPEC)
2150 Maple St
Vancouver, BC, V6J 3T3
736-7732

NEXT PAGE: You never know what you'll discover when touring by bike.

Route Finder

Column Explanations

L = Length (km); oXX = one way

EG= Cumulative Elevation Gain (m), rounded up to nearest 25 m; (XXX) means avoidable—see note *.

F = Fitness: overall assessment of physical challenge (relative to the other routes in this book) based on length, and more heavily on cumulative elevation gain, steepness of hills, and surface quality where 1=short and flat and 5=long and/or with more elevation gain and/or steeper hills and/or rougher surface

T = Traffic Hazard Factor: a subjective judgement (relative to the other routes in this book) based on traffic density, traffic speed, and road narrowness where 1=no or little traffic and 5=sections with more traffic challenge. It is weighted heavily towards the worst parts of the route; so, for example, although a route might be rated T5 overall because of several busy sections, much of it might actually be fairly car-free. Of course the time of day, day of the week, and season will affect these ratings. (**Note**: percentages below estimated to nearest 10%)

P = Paved percentage of route

M = Mountain Bike; n = not required, s = suggested, r = recommended, o = mountain biking options

R = Percentage of route that runs through rural, wilderness, or park-like surroundings

Significant Features/Highlights Coding

(note: one attraction may account for more than one code; e.g. a park with walking trails and a fish hatchery)

1. Architecture (unusual and/or old buildings and structures)
2. Art/Craft Gallery (or shop)
3. Berries/Fruit (roadside stand, U-pick, or wild)
4. Campsites (mostly formal)
5. Historic Site (or emphasis)
6. Technology/Machinery/Industry (e.g. dam, fishboats, aircraft museum)
7. Museum (all kinds)
8. Nature (e.g., birdwatching, fish hatchery, tall trees, bog, etc.)
9. Picnic Site (formal and informal)
10. Scenery (mostly vistas, but including gardens and pretty parks)
11. Shoreline and Riverbank
12. Swimming Beach
13. Walking/Hiking Trail
14. Park (or similar) of note

No.	Title	Page	L	EG	F	T	P	M	R	Highlights
VANCOUVER, BURNABY, NEW WESTMINSTER										
V1	Stanley Park Seawall	18	10.1	0	1	1	100	n	100	5,8,9,10,11,12,13,14
V2	False Creek	22	8.1	0	1	3	100	n	0	1,2,5,6,7,9,10,11
V3	Kitsilano Shores	26	13.6	75	2	3	80	n	40	1,3,5,6,7,9,10,11,12,14
V4	Mansions of Shaughnessy	30	8.9	100	2	3	100	n	0	1,5,9
V5	Rural Southlands and Point Grey	34	22.7	200	4	3	90	n	30	1,6,8,9,10,11,12,14
V6	UBC and Marpole	40	31.2	225	4	3	100	o	40	1,5,7,9,10,11,12,13,14
V7	South Vancouver Gardens	44	14.7	125	3	3	100	n	20	1,5,9,10,13,14
V8	Killarney Milk Run	48	14.6	150	3	3	100	n	10	1,5,6,9,10,12,13,14
V9	Strathcona/Waterfront	52	17.6	125	2	4	100	n	0	1,2,5,6,7,9,10,14

*   This route is actually described downwards—the figure in parentheses is the climb in the reverse direction (slightly less if you take the road up). As well, though riding this trail uphill is definitely more challenging, the way down also requires a fair degree of riding skill.

Index

V

W

Personal Road Log

ABOUT THE AUTHOR

A resident of the Lower Mainland for most of his life, Volker Bodegom has been an avid cyclist since the tender age of eight and now uses his bicycle to meet most of his local transportation needs. Volker is a volunteer with several environmental and cycling groups, including the Better Environmentally Sound Transportation Association (BEST) and the Bicycling Association of BC. He is active in cycling advocacy and has previously written articles on cycling events and environmental issues. Volker's varied interests also include hiking, backpacking, orienteering, electronics, photography and cross-country skiing. *Bicycling Vancouver* is his first book.